Navigating the Labyrinth

An Executive Guide to Data Management

By Laura Sebastian-Coleman

For DAMA International

Technics Publications

Published by:

 TECHNICS PUBLICATIONS
TECHNOLOGY / LEADERSHIP

2 Lindsley Road
Basking Ridge, NJ 07920 USA

https://www.TechnicsPub.com

Edited by Lauren McCafferty
Cover design by Lorena Molinari

First Printing 2018

Copyright © 2018 by Laura Sebastian-Coleman, Ph.D.

ISBN, print ed.   9781634623759
ISBN, Kindle ed.   9781634623766
ISBN, ePub ed.   9781634623773
ISBN, PDF ed.   9781634623780

Library of Congress Control Number: 2018942062

Contents

To meditate is to sail a course, to navigate, among problems many of which we are in the process of clearing up. After each one looms another, whose shores are even more attractive, more suggestive. Certainly, it requires strength and perseverance to get to windward of problems, but there is no greater delight than to reach new shores, and even to sail, as Camoëns says, "through seas that keel has never cut before."

— José Ortega y Gasset, *Man and People*

Foreword

Data management professionals have long struggled to balance their work with sharing *why* data is so important, assisting with the culture change needed to bring data to the forefront, and finally soliciting leadership commitment to improvement. This balancing act is even more important today as the sheer volume, variety, and velocity of data increases exponentially.

As good data people, we turn to books to help us. More specifically, we turn to the DAMA-DMBOK2. The tome of 600-odd pages is a mammoth read and often dives deep into important data management concepts. Great for building your data management framework, but pretty unrealistic when trying to get the point across to the boss.

We need something between the proverbial elevator pitch and the DAMA-DMBOK2. Something that simply and pragmatically enables leadership to understand the importance of effective data management – not only for the success of the organization, but also for their own personal success. Something that doesn't weigh more than a small child, is small enough to be carried around in a laptop bag and provides the executive précis (the cliff notes) of data management.

And this is what Laura has so aptly managed to create in *Navigating the Labyrinth*. It's a pocket edition of the DAMA-DMBOK2, something that every data management professional should get two copies of – one for themselves and one for their manager (or, better yet, for the executive most likely to understand data as opportunity). This book will become their go-to reference and their lifeline. It will become dog-eared from use, notes will appear in the margins, and peers will all look longingly at it and wish for their own copy.

DAMA International is incredibly proud of the DAMA-DMBOK2. Many years of work and well over 100 people have put huge effort into creating what we believe is "the" framework for data management. Now *Navigating the Labyrinth* is poised to break that executive barrier and deliver data management where it belongs – right up there with all the other business imperatives.

On a personal level, I am proud of the DAMA-DMBOK2, but I am even more proud of this lightweight yet incredibly valuable addition to the DAMA fold. I believe that for each person who buys and reads the DMBOK2, it's very likely that three to four or more will buy and read *Navigating the Labyrinth*. Thank you, Laura.

Sue Geuens
President, DAMA International

Introduction

You've sensed it, you've read it, you've seen it. Reliable, well-managed data is critical to organizational success in the twenty-first century. Whatever sector you work in – financial services, health care, insurance, manufacturing, technology, retail, education, and beyond – your organization requires data to transact business and serve customers. This data not only fuels your business processes; it also provides you the business intelligence needed to measure organizational success. As importantly, the data your organization produces can be mined for insights about current operations—insights you can apply to improve your processes and advance your organization's strategy.

But reliable data is not produced by accident. In today's complex world, well-managed data depends on planning and design, governance of business and technical processes, and the commitment of your organization to high-quality results. It also means ensuring that information about customers, products, and business operations is kept safe and secure, so that it cannot be used for criminal or malicious purposes.

Reliable data depends on successful execution of the functions and activities that comprise the field of data management. These are described in detail in DAMA International's *Data Management Body of Knowledge* (known as the *DMBOK2*). Understanding the breadth and depth of functions that make up data management can be daunting. At first glance, they can appear quite complicated (see Figure 1).

Navigating the Labyrinth: An Executive Guide to Data Management gives you a perspective that reduces this complexity. Based on the *DMBOK2*, it provides a high-level overview of how data should be managed to support organizational success. It also explains what can get in the way of this success. Understanding the principles and best practices for data management will help you identify and act on your organization's opportunities to get more value from its data.

Figure 1: Data Management Functions (DMBOK2, p. 44)

The first four chapters provide an overview of data management:

- **Chapter 1: The Importance of Managing Data** – Explains what data management is, and how managing data as an asset can help your organization.

- **Chapter 2: Data Management Challenges** – Outlines why managing data differs from managing other assets and resources.

- **Chapter 3: DAMA's Data Management Principles** – Explains principles of effective data management that will help you overcome the challenges presented by data; introduces the concept of evolving your organization's data management practices based on a maturity model.

- **Chapter 4: Data Ethics** – Describes the principles underlying an ethical approach to data management; explains how this approach to data handling can help prevent your organization's data from being used in ways that harm your customers, your reputation, or the wider community.

The next four chapters review the mechanics of managing the data lifecycle:

- **Chapter 5: Data Governance** – Explains the role of data governance in providing oversight for data; highlights the ways an organization can implement governance practices to make better operational and strategic decisions about data.

- **Chapter 6: Planning and Design in the Data Lifecycle** – Describes the role of architecture and data modeling in data management, and the importance of planning and design in managing the overall lifecycle of data.

- **Chapter 7: Enabling and Maintaining Data** – Provides and overview of activities related to obtaining, integrating, and storing data and enabling its currency and access over time. These activities include applying design concepts to create reliable, performant, and secure warehouses, marts, and other data storage environments, where different types of data can be integrated and made available for a wide range of uses.

- **Chapter 8: Using and Enhancing Data** – Describes the ways that data can be used to create new data to bring value to an organization. Data enhancement adds both value and complexity to the data lifecycle. It requires organizations to plan for and cultivate the organic growth of data.

The following three chapters cover the foundational activities required to help build trust in data and ensure the organization can get value from its data over time:

- **Chapter 9: Data Protection, Privacy, Security and Risk Management** – Describes how to manage risks related to data, especially those connected with potential breaches or malicious uses of data.

- **Chapter 10: Metadata Management** – Provides an overview of how to manage Metadata, that critical sub-set of data which contains the knowledge required to use and maintain the rest of your data.

- **Chapter 11: Data Quality Management** – Presents techniques for ensuring that your organization's data is fit for its intended purposes and enables your organization to meet its strategic goals. These techniques apply the principles of product management to data, and are aligned with the principles of data management described in Chapter 3.

Each chapter concludes with assertions about what you need to know about these topics. **Chapter 12 What to do Now** concludes the book with an approach to re-directing your organization's data management practices through a current state assessment, a defined roadmap, and a commitment to organizational change management.

DAMA recognizes that to most executives, data management can seem obscure, complicated, and highly technical. You don't have time to learn all the detail or cut through the hype. But if your organization depends on data – and most organizations do – then you have a critical role to play in enabling success. Reliable data management takes organizational commitment, and organizational commitment comes from leadership. DAMA hopes that by navigating the labyrinth of data management, you can develop opportunities for your organization to get more value from its data. This book will explain the fundamentals and help you understand why they are important, so you can focus attention on how to build trust in your organization's data through efficient and effective practices.

CHAPTER 1

The Importance of
Managing Data

Even before the rise of information technology, information and knowledge have been keys to competitive advantage. Organizations that have reliable, high-quality information about their customers, products, services, and operations can make better decisions than those without data (or with unreliable data). But producing high-quality data and managing it in ways that enable it to be used effectively is not a simple process.

This chapter will review the following concepts, which are important to any organization that wants to improve its data management capabilities:

- Data's ubiquity – the fact that almost every organizational process creates or consumes data or both
- Data's value as an asset
- Why it is important to understand data management separately from technology management
- The range of activities and functions involved with managing data

DATA IS EVERYWHERE

Organizations have always needed to manage their data, but advances in technology have expanded the scope of this management need. Data is pervasive across organizations. Almost every business process – from setting up customers, to transacting purchases, to contacting customers for feedback and services – uses data as input and produces data as output. Most of this data is in electronic form, which means that it is malleable: it can be stored in large quantities, manipulated, integrated, and aggregated for different uses, including business intelligence and predictive analytics. It also provides evidence of an organization's compliance (or lack of compliance) with laws and regulations.

Technical changes have enabled organizations to use data in new ways to create products, share information, create knowledge, and improve organizational success. But the rapid growth of technology and with it human capacity to produce, capture, and mine data for meaning has intensified the need to manage data effectively.

DATA AS AN ASSET

An *asset* is an economic resource, that can be owned or controlled, and that holds or produces value. Assets are often thought of as property, but with the strong implication that they can be converted to money. Data is widely recognized as an enterprise asset, although many organizations still struggle to manage data as an asset. For example, data is not yet accounted for in most organizations' balance sheets.

If asked, many senior executives would say that their organization's data is a valuable asset. It is not only necessary to business operations, but it can also provide insight into customers, products, and services. Nevertheless, research shows that very few organizations treat their data as an asset.[1] For many it can even be a liability. Failure to manage data is similar to failure to manage capital. It results in waste and lost opportunity. Poorly-managed data presents ethical as well as security risks.

Even executives who recognize data as an asset may not be able to describe exactly what that means, since data differs from other assets in important ways. Nevertheless, the primary driver for data management is to enable organizations to get value from their data, just as effective management of financial and physical assets enables organizations to get value from those assets. Deriving value from data does not happen in a vacuum or by accident. It requires organizational commitment and leadership, as well as management.

DATA MANAGEMENT VS. TECHNOLOGY MANAGEMENT

Data management is the development, execution, and supervision of plans, policies, programs, and practices that deliver, control, protect, and enhance the value of data and information assets, throughout their lifecycle.

You may think, "Isn't that what our information technology department already does?" Unfortunately, no. IT usually does not focus on data. IT focuses technology, technological processes, the people who build applications, and the tools they use to do so. Historically, IT has not focused on the data that is created by or stored in the applications it builds. If anything, IT has tended to be dismissive of the data itself (because IT professes to have no control over data) – despite the fact that many data management functions are part of IT.

Though data management is highly dependent on technology and intersects with technology management, it involves separate activities that are independent from specific technical tools and processes.

---

[1] Evans & Price, 2012; Laney 2018.

Given this definition, what does data management actually involve? What does it mean to manage data effectively? Like all forms of management, data management involves planning and coordinating resources and activities in order to meet organizational objectives. The activities themselves range from the highly technical, like ensuring that large databases are accessible, performant, and secure, to the highly strategic, like determining how to expand market share through innovative uses of data. These management activities must strive to make high-quality, reliable data available to the organization, while ensuring this data is accessible to authorized users and protected from misuse.

DATA MANAGEMENT ACTIVITIES

Data management activities can be understood in groups: some focus on governance to ensure the organization makes sound, consistent decisions about data; others are foundational and focus on enabling the management, maintenance, and use of data over time; and some focus on managing the data lifecycle, from obtaining data through disposing of it (see Figure 2).

- **Governance activities** help control data development and reduce risks associated with data use, while at the same time, enabling an organization to leverage data strategically. These activities establish a system of decision rights and responsibilities for data, so that an organization can make consistent decisions across business verticals.[2] Governance activities include things like:

    o Defining data strategy
    o Setting policy
    o Stewarding data
    o Defining the value of data to the organization

---

[2] The Data Governance Institute. https://bit.ly/1ef0tnb.

- o Preparing the organization to get more value from its data by
  - Maturing its data management practices
  - Evolving the organization's mindset around data though culture change

- **Lifecycle activities** focus on planning and designing for data, enabling its use, ensuring it is effectively maintained, and actually using it. Use of data often results in enhancements and innovations, which have their own lifecycle requirements. Lifecycle activities include:

  - o Data Architecture
  - o Data Modeling
  - o Building and managing data warehouses and marts
  - o Integrating data for use by business intelligence analysts and data scientists
  - o Managing the lifecycle of highly critical shared data, like Reference Data and Master Data

- **Foundational activities** are required for consistent management of data over time. Integral to the entire data lifecycle, these activities include:

  - o Ensuring data is protected
  - o Managing Metadata, the knowledge required to understand and use data
  - o Managing the quality of data

Foundational activities must be accounted for as part of planning and design, and they must be carried out operationally. These activities are also supported by and integral to the success of governance structures.

DATA MANAGEMENT KNOWLEDGE AREAS

The work of data management is carried out by people working in data management functions or knowledge areas, which require different skills and expertise (see Figure 3).

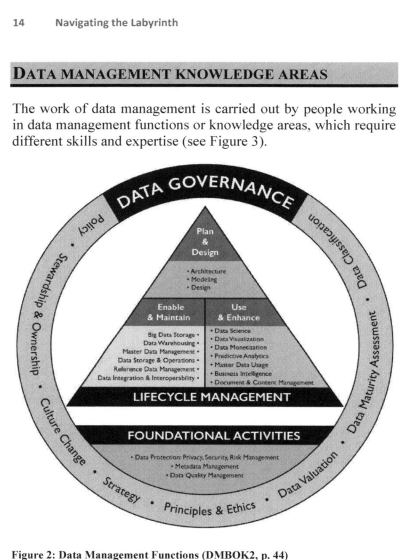

Figure 2: Data Management Functions (DMBOK2, p. 44)

DAMA International has defined eleven knowledge areas:

- **Data Governance** provides direction and oversight for data management activities and functions by establishing a system of decision rights and responsibilities for data. These rights and responsibilities should account for the needs of the enterprise as a whole.

- **Data Architecture** defines the blueprint for managing data assets by aligning with organizational strategy and establishing designs to meet strategic data requirements.

- **Data Modeling and Design** is the process of discovering, analyzing, representing, and communicating data requirements in a precise form called the data model.

- **Data Storage and Operations** includes the design, implementation, and support of stored data to maximize its value. Operations provide support throughout the data lifecycle from planning for to disposal of data.

- **Data Security** ensures that data privacy and confidentiality are maintained, that data is not breached, and that data is accessed appropriately.

- **Data Integration & Interoperability** includes processes related to the movement and consolidation of data within and between data stores, applications, and organizations.

- **Document and Content Management** includes planning, implementation, and control activities to manage the lifecycle of data and information found in a range of unstructured media, especially documents needed to support legal and regulatory compliance requirements.

- **Reference and Master Data Management** includes ongoing reconciliation and maintenance of core critical shared data to enable consistent use across systems of the most accurate, timely, and relevant version of truth about essential business entities.

- **Data Warehousing and Business Intelligence** includes the planning, implementation, and control processes to manage decision support data and to enable knowledge workers to get value from data via analysis and reporting.

- **Metadata Management** includes planning, implementation, and control activities to enable access to high-quality, integrated Metadata, including definitions, models, data flows, and other information critical to understanding data and the systems through which it is created, maintained, and accessed.

- **Data Quality Management** includes the planning and implementation of quality management techniques to measure, assess, and improve the fitness of data for use within an organization.

These knowledge areas represent activities at the core of data management. Any organization trying to get value from its data must engage in them. But they are also evolving. Changes in our capacity to create and use data mean that other concepts could also be considered data management "knowledge areas" (such as data ethics, data science, Big Data management, and emergent technologies).

Data management professionals working in these knowledge areas help an organization:

- Understand and support the information needs of the enterprise and its stakeholders, including customers, employees, and business partners
- Capture, store, and ensure the integrity and quality of data to enable its use by the enterprise
- Ensure the security, privacy, and confidentiality of data by preventing inappropriate access, manipulation, or use

WHAT YOU NEED TO KNOW

- The goal of data management is to enable an organization to get more value from its data.

- In a world dependent on data, reliable data management practices are becoming more critical.

- Data management includes governance, foundational, and lifecycle activities.

- Data management involves a range of skills – from strategic to highly technical.

- Data management practices are rapidly evolving as business needs and technological capacity evolve.

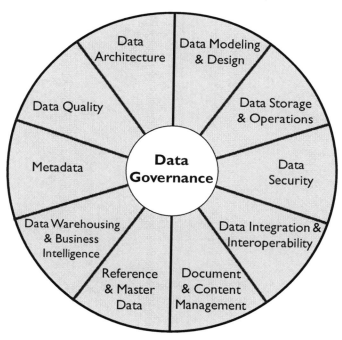

Copyright © 2017 by DAMA International

Figure 3: The DAMA DMBOK2 Data Management Framework (DMBOK2, p.36)

CHAPTER 2

Data Management Challenges

Data is both an operational necessity and an asset. Effective data management can enable an organization to get more value from its data. Managing any asset requires working to get value from it, managing its lifecycle, and managing it across an enterprise. But the unique characteristics of data put a different spin on these functions. This chapter will cover the following concepts related to these challenges:

- Managing data as an asset
  - Data differs from other assets
  - Data represents risk
  - Poor quality data costs time and money
  - Data valuation is not standardized

- Managing the data lifecycle
  - Data management includes managing data's lifecycle

- o   Different kinds of data have different lifecycle requirements
- o   Metadata must be managed as part of the data lifecycle

- • Managing data across an enterprise
  - o   Data management is often confused with information technology management
  - o   Data management is cross-functional and requires a range of skills
  - o   Data management requires an enterprise perspective and leadership commitment

DATA DIFFERS FROM OTHER ASSETS

Data has unique characteristics that make it different from other assets.[3] Physical assets can be pointed to, touched, and moved around. Financial assets are accounted for on a balance sheet. But data is different. Data is not tangible. Yet it is durable; it does not wear out. Data is easy to copy and transport. But it is not easy to reproduce if it is lost or destroyed. Because it is not consumed when used, it can even be stolen without being gone. Data is dynamic and can be used for multiple purposes. The same data can even be used by multiple people at the same time – something that is impossible with physical or financial assets. Many uses of data beget more data.

These differences make it challenging simply to keep track of data, much less put a monetary value on data. Without this monetary value, it can be difficult to measure how data contributes to organizational success. These differences also raise other issues that affect data management, such as:

---

[3] This section derives from Redman, Thomas. *Data Quality for the Information Age* (1996) pp. 41-42, 232-36; and *Data Driven* (2008), Chapter One, "The Wondrous and Perilous Properties of Data and Information."

- Inventorying how much data an organization has
- Defining data ownership and accountability
- Protecting against the misuse of data
- Managing risks associated with data
- Defining and enforcing quality standards for data

DATA REPRESENTS RISK

Data not only represents value and opportunity; it also presents risks. Inaccurate, incomplete, or out-of-date data obviously represents risk because its information is not right. But data presents other risks, including:

- **Misuse**: If data consumers do not have sufficient and correct information (Metadata) about the data they use, then there is a risk of data being misused or misunderstood.

- **Unreliability**: If data quality and reliability have not been established through standards and measurements, then there is a risk that unreliable data will be used to make decisions.

- **Inappropriate use**: If data is not protected and secured, then there is a risk that data will be used by unauthorized people for unauthorized purposes.

The fact that data can be easily copied and replicated means it can be breached without being 'gone' from its rightful owners. Moreover, because data represents people, products, and money, legislators and regulators have recognized the potential uses and abuses of information and have put in place laws intended to mitigate obvious risks. For example:

- Sarbanes-Oxley in the US focuses on controls over accuracy and validity of financial transaction data from transaction to balance sheet

- Solvency II in the EU focuses on data lineage and the quality of data underpinning risk models and capital adequacy in the insurance sector

- Throughout the world, data privacy regulations describe obligations toward the handling of personal identifying data (e.g., name, addresses, religious affiliation, or sexual orientation) and privacy (access or restriction to this information). Examples include:
    o Health Insurance Portability and Accountability Act (HIPPA) in the US
    o Personal Information Protection and Electronic Documents Act (PIPEDA) in Canada
    o The General Data Protection Regulation (GDPR) in the EU

Consumers are also more aware of how their data might be used. For example, when making purchases on a website, they expect not only smoother and more efficient operation of processes, but also protection of their information and respect for their privacy. Organizations that do not protect their customers' data may not have those customers for long.

POOR QUALITY DATA COSTS MONEY

Ensuring that data is of high quality is central to data management. If data does not meet the needs of its consumers – if it is not 'fit for purpose' – then the effort to collect, store, secure, and enable access to it is wasted. To ensure data meets business needs, data management teams must work with data consumers to define the characteristics that make data of high quality.

Most uses of data involve learning from it in order to apply that learning and create value. For example, understanding customer habits in order to improve a product or service; assessing organizational performance or market trends, in order to develop a better business strategy, etc. Poor quality data will have a negative impact on these decisions.

As importantly, poor quality data is simply costly to any organization. Estimates differ, but experts think organizations spend between 10-30% of revenue handling data quality issues. IBM estimated the cost of poor quality data in the US in 2016 was $3.1 Trillion.[4]

Many of the costs of poor quality data are hidden and indirect and therefore hard to measure. Others, like fines, are direct and easy to calculate. Costs come from:

- Scrap and rework
- Work-arounds and hidden correction processes
- Organizational inefficiencies or low productivity
- Organizational conflict
- Low job satisfaction
- Customer dissatisfaction
- Opportunity costs, including the inability to innovate
- Compliance costs or fines
- Reputational and public relations costs

The corresponding benefits of high quality data include:

- Improved customer experience
- Higher productivity
- Reduced risk
- Ability to act on opportunities
- Increased revenue
- Competitive advantage gained from insights on customers, products, processes, and opportunities
- Competitive advantage gained from demonstrable data security and data quality

As these costs and benefits imply, managing data quality is not a one-time thing. Producing high-quality data requires planning,

---

[4] Reported in Redman, Thomas. "Bad Data Costs U.S. $3 Trillion per Year." Harvard Business Review. 22 September 2016. https://bit.ly/2cUsIR3.

commitment, and a mindset that builds quality into processes and systems. All data management functions can influence the quality of data, for good or bad, so they all must account for data quality as they execute their work.

DATA VALUATION IS NOT STANDARDIZED

Since each organization's data is unique to itself, it can be difficult to put a monetary value on data. How much does it cost to collect and manage the history of a customer's purchases? How much would it cost to reconstruct that history if the data were lost?

Still, putting monetary value on data is useful because it informs decisions about data and becomes the basis of understanding the value on data management activities.[5] One approach to data valuation is to define general cost and benefit categories that can be applied consistently within an organization. Sample categories include:

- Cost of obtaining and storing data
- Cost of replacing data if it were lost
- Impact to the organization if data were missing
- Potential costs of risks associated with data
- Cost of risk mitigation
- Cost of improving data
- Benefits of higher quality data
- What competitors would pay for data
- What the data could be sold for
- Expected revenue from innovative uses of data

Data asset valuation must also recognize that the value of data is contextual (i.e., what is of value to one organization may not be

---

[5] For case studies and examples, see Aiken, Peter and Billings, Juanita. *Monetizing Data Management* (2014) and Laney, Douglas, *Infonomics: How to Monetize, Manage, and Measure Information as an Asset for Competitive Advantage* (2018).

of value to another) and often temporal (i.e., what was valuable yesterday may not be valuable today). Despite this, within an organization, certain types of data, such as customer data, are likely to be consistently valuable over time, so most organizations focus first on ensuring the quality of this highly critical data.

DATA MANAGEMENT MEANS MANAGING DATA'S LIFECYCLE

One reason people conflate data management with technology management is that they often see data only in one place: the application from which they access it. They do not recognize that data can be separate from the applications where it is created or stored and that data has a lifecycle. The data lifecycle is based on the product lifecycle. It focuses on ensuring that data is created, moved, and maintained in ways that make it is usable by the people and processes that require it. Even though data and technology are intertwined, the data lifecycle should not be confused with the systems development lifecycle (SDLC), which focuses on completing projects on time and within budget.

Conceptually, the data lifecycle is easy to describe (see Figure 4). It includes processes that create or obtain data, those that move, transform, and store it and enable it to be maintained and shared, and those that use or apply it, as well as those that dispose of it.[6] Data is rarely static. Throughout its lifecycle, data may be cleansed, transformed, merged, enhanced, or aggregated. Data often moves horizontally within organization. As data is used or enhanced, new data is created, so the lifecycle has internal iterations and the 'same' data may have different lifecycle requirements in different parts of an organization.

---

[6] McGilvray, 2008; English, 1999. DAMA's lifecycle depiction is based on McGilvray's formulation, POSMAD – Plan, Obtain, Store & Share, Maintain, Apply, Dispose – which has proved a very valuable model, especially in the data quality space.

Complexity is added to the concept of the data lifecycle by the fact that different kinds of data have different lifecycle requirements. For example, transactional data can be controlled largely through enforcement of basic rules, while Master Data requires curation. Still some principles apply to the lifecycle of any data:

- **Creation and usage are the most critical points in the data lifecycle**[7]: Data management must be executed with an understanding of how data is produced, or obtained, as well as how data is used. It costs money to produce data. Data is valuable only when it is consumed or applied.

- **Data quality must be managed throughout the data lifecycle**: Because the quality of data can be impacted by a range of lifecycle events, quality must be planned for as part of the data lifecycle. It is not an add-on, or something to be 'done later.'

- **Metadata quality must be managed through the data lifecycle**: Metadata is a type of data that is used to describe other data. As such, it is critical to all data management functions. Metadata is often created as part of the lifecycle of other data and should be seen as a product (rather than a by-product) of that lifecycle. Metadata quality must be managed in the same way as the quality of other data.

- **Data Security must be managed throughout the data lifecycle**: Data management includes ensuring that data is secure and that risks associated with data are mitigated. Data that requires protection must be protected throughout its lifecycle, from creation to disposal.

---

[7] McGilvray (2008) points out that there are costs at all points in the data lifecycle, but value is created only when data is used. See also Redman (2008).

- **Data management efforts should focus on the most critical data**: Organizations produce a lot of data, much of which is never actually used.[8] Trying to manage every piece of data is neither possible nor desirable. Lifecycle management requires focusing on an organization's most critical data and minimizing data ROT (i.e., data that is redundant, obsolete, or trivial).[9]

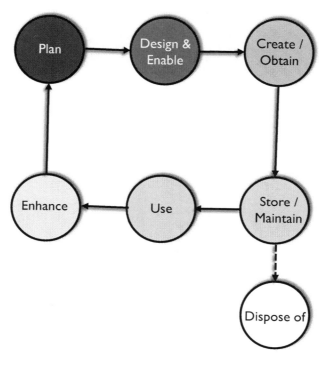

Figure 4: The Data Lifecycle (DMBOK2, p. 29)

---

[8] Figures differ, but a quick Google search of "What percentage of data is unused?" produces three that are somewhat shocking: 97% according to Gartner (25 January 2018), 85% according to Veritas (15 March 2016), and 73% according to Inc.com (12 April 2018).

[9] Aiken, 2014.

DIFFERENT KINDS OF DATA HAVE DIFFERENT LIFECYCLE REQUIREMENTS

Managing data is made more complicated by the fact that different types of data have different lifecycle management requirements. Data can be classified by the function it serves (e.g., transactional data, Reference Data, Master Data, Metadata; alternatively, category data, resource data, event data, detailed transaction data) or by content (e.g., data domains, subject areas) or by format or by the level of protection the data requires. Data can also be classified by how and where it is stored or accessed.

Because different types of data have different requirements, are associated with different risks, and play different roles within an organization, many of the tools of data management are focused on aspects of classification and control.[10] For example, Master Data has different uses and consequently different management requirements than does transactional data.

METADATA MUST BE MANAGED AS PART OF THE DATA LIFECYCLE

Data management professionals are passionate about Metadata because they realize how important it is. Yet it is a truism among them that one should never use the word *Metadata* when speaking with executives. "Their eyes will glaze over!" We'll take that chance here because certain forms of Metadata are not simply critical to data management—they are essential to it. You cannot manage data without Metadata.

Metadata includes a range of information that allows people to understand data and the systems that contain data. Metadata describes what data an organization has, what it represents, how it is classified, where it came from, how it moves within the organization, how it evolves through use, who can and cannot use it, and whether it is of high quality.

---

[10] Bryce, 2005.

The challenge is not only that you need Metadata to manage data, but that Metadata is a form of data and needs to be managed as such. Organizations that do not manage their data well generally do not manage their Metadata at all. The answer to this challenge is that Metadata management often provides a starting point for improvements in data management overall.

DATA MANAGEMENT IS OFTEN CONFUSED WITH INFORMATION TECHNOLOGY MANAGEMENT

Because almost all of today's data is stored electronically, data management is closely linked with technology management. They need to be seen in relation to one another, because decisions about technology impact many facets of how data is managed. But data management, which focuses on ensuring that the data itself is usable and trustworthy, differs from technology management, which focuses on building and maintaining infrastructure, systems, and applications.

The two are fundamentally connected by the fact that these systems and applications often automate business processes that collect or create data and different technological choices will put different constraints on the data itself. Both data management and technology management requirements should be rooted in business processes that create or use data and the needs of the people and processes that consume data.

In many organizations there is ongoing tension between the drive to build new technology and the desire to have more reliable data – as if the two were opposed to each other instead of necessary to each other. Successful data management requires sound decisions about technology, but managing technology is not the same as managing data. Organizations need to understand the impact of technology on data, in order to prevent technological temptation from driving their decisions about data. Instead, data requirements aligned with business strategy should drive decisions about technology.

DATA MANAGEMENT REQUIRES A RANGE OF SKILLS

Managing data involves a set of interconnected processes aligned with the data lifecycle. Though many organizations see data management as an information technology function, it actually requires a wide range of people with a diverse set of skills working in different parts of an organization. Data management is a complex process because it is executed throughout an organization. Data is managed in different places within an organization by teams that have responsibility for different phases of the data lifecycle. Data management requires:

- Business process skills to understand and plan for the creation of reliable data

- Design skills to plan for systems where data will be stored or used

- Highly technical skills to administer hardware and build software where data is maintained

- Data analysis skills to understand issues and problems discovered in data

- Analytic skills to interpret data and apply it to new problems

- Language skills to bring consensus to definitions and models so that people can understand data

- Strategic thinking to see opportunities to use data to serve customers and meet goals

The challenge is getting people with this range of skills and perspectives to recognize how the pieces fit together and how their work intersects with the work of other parts of the organization so that they successfully collaborate and achieve common goals.

DATA MANAGEMENT REQUIRES AN ENTERPRISE PERSPECTIVE

The footprint of data management is as large as the organization that creates and uses data. Data is one of the 'horizontals' of an organization. It moves across verticals, such as sales, marketing, and operations. Or at least it should. Ideally, data should be managed from an enterprise perspective. However, getting to an enterprise perspective is challenging.

Most organizations break work down by business units or functions, each of which may develop its own applications to perform its work. Because data is often viewed simply as a by-product of operational processes (for example, sales transaction records are the by-product of the selling process, not an end in themselves), it is not always planned for beyond the immediate need. It may not even be recognized as something that other people and processes use.

Unless enterprise data standards are established and enforced, there will be differences in how data is defined and created in different areas. For example, take something as seemingly simple as a Social Security Number (SSN), a US identifier for individuals. If one application captures SSN as a numeric value and another captures it in a text field, SSN data will be formatted differently. This can result in problems like dropping leading zeros on SSNs. Formatting differences, differences in the granularity of data, and differences about which attributes are mandatory to capture – all of these differences present obstacles to integrating data from diverse applications. Obstacles to integration limit the value an organization can get from its data.

Organizations that view data as a product that they create or purchase will make better decisions about how to manage it throughout its lifecycle. These decisions require recognizing:

- The ways data connects business processes that might otherwise be seen as separate

- The relationship between business processes and the technology that supports them

- The design and architecture of systems and the data they produce and store

- The ways data might be used to advance organizational strategy

Planning for better data requires a strategic approach to architecture, modeling, and other design functions. It also depends on strategic collaboration between business and IT leadership. And, of course, it demands the ability to execute effectively on individual projects. The challenge is that there are usually organizational pressures, as well as the perennial pressures of time and money, that get in the way of better planning. Organizations must balance long- and short-term goals as they execute their strategy. Having clarity about the trade-offs leads to better decisions.

WHAT YOU NEED TO KNOW

- Data is a valuable asset but also represents risk. An organization can begin to understand the value of its data by recognizing both the costs of poor quality data and the benefits of high-quality data.

- Data has unique characteristics that make it challenging to manage.

- The best approach to addressing these challenges is to manage data across its lifecycle and to take an enterprise perspective.

- Failure to manage the data lifecycle is costly, though many costs are hidden.

- Managing data across its lifecycle requires planning, skill, and teamwork.

CHAPTER 3

DAMA's Data Management Principles

Managing data presents unique challenges connected to the nature of data itself. Even with its unique characteristics, data management still shares characteristics with other forms of management. It involves knowing what data an organization has and what might be accomplished with it, then determining how best to use data assets to reach organizational goals. Like other management processes, it must balance strategic and operational needs. It must also account for the unique properties of data reviewed in Chapter 2.

To help organizations strike this balance, DAMA has developed a set of principles that recognize the challenges of data management and help guide data management practice.

At the highest level, these principles boil down to four assertions (see Figure 5) which we will review in this chapter:

- Data is valuable

- Data management requirements are business requirements

- Data management depends on diverse skills

- Data management is lifecycle management

DAMA's data management principles provide a lens through which to understand how your organization manages its data. After reviewing their implications, we will look at them in the context of data management maturity. A maturity model defines a progression of increasing control over a set of processes. When an organization gains an understanding of process characteristics, it can put in place a plan to improve its capabilities. It can also measure improvement and compare itself to competitors or partners, guided by the levels of the model. Data management maturity models describe details of data management processes that can be used for this type of evaluation. We will return to the concept of data management maturity in Chapter 12 when we discuss how to assess the current state of your organization.

DATA IS VALUABLE

- **Data is an asset with unique properties**: Data is an asset, but it differs from other assets in important ways that impact how it is managed. The most obvious of these properties is that data is not consumed when it is used, as are financial and physical assets.

- **The value of data can and should be expressed in economic terms**: Calling data an asset implies that it has value. While there are techniques for measuring data's qualitative and quantitative value, there are not yet standards for doing so. Organizations that want to make better decisions about their data should develop consistent ways to quantify that value. They should also measure both the costs of low quality data and the benefits of high-quality data.

- **Effective data management requires leadership commitment**: Data management involves a complex set of processes that, to be effective, require coordination, collaboration, and commitment. Getting there requires not only management skills, but also the vision and purpose that comes from committed leadership.

DATA MANAGEMENT REQUIREMENTS ARE BUSINESS REQUIREMENTS

- **Managing data means managing the quality of data**: Ensuring that data is fit for purpose is a primary goal of data management. To manage quality, organizations must ensure they understand stakeholders' requirements for quality and measure data against these requirements.

- **It takes Metadata to manage data**: Managing any asset requires having data about that asset (number of employees, accounting codes, etc.). The data used to manage and use data is called Metadata. Because data cannot be held or touched, to understand what it is and how to use it requires definition and knowledge in the form of Metadata. Metadata originates from a range of processes related to data creation, processing, and use, including architecture, modeling, stewardship, governance, data quality management, systems development, IT and business operations, and analytics.

- **It takes planning to manage data**: Even small organizations can have complex technical and business process landscapes. Data is created in many places and is moved between places for use. To coordinate work and keep the end results aligned requires planning from an architectural and process perspective.

- **Data management requirements must drive Information Technology decisions**: Data and data management are deeply intertwined with information technology and information technology management. Managing data requires an approach that ensures technology serves, rather than drives, an organization's strategic data needs.

DATA MANAGEMENT IS LIFECYCLE MANAGEMENT

- **Data management is lifecycle management**: Data has a lifecycle and managing data requires managing its lifecycle. Because data begets more data, the data lifecycle itself can be very complex. Data management practices need to account for the evolving lifecycle of data.

- **Different types of data have different lifecycle characteristics**: And for this reason, they have different management requirements. Data management practices have to recognize these differences and be flexible enough to meet different kinds of data lifecycle requirements.

- **Managing data includes managing the risks associated with data**: In addition to being an asset, data also represents risk to an organization. Data can be lost, stolen, or misused. Organizations must consider the ethical implications of their uses of data. Data-related risks must be managed as part of the data lifecycle.

DATA MANAGEMENT DEPENDS ON DIVERSE SKILLS

- **Data management is cross-functional:** A single team cannot manage all of an organization's data. Doing so requires a range of skills and expertise. Data management requires both technical and non-technical skills and the ability to collaborate.

- **Data management requires an enterprise perspective**: Data management has local applications, but it must be applied across the enterprise to be as effective as possible. This is one reason why data management and data governance are intertwined.

- **Data management must account for a range of perspectives**: Data is fluid and changing. Data management must constantly evolve to keep up with the ways data is created and used and the data consumers who use it.

DATA MANAGEMENT PRINCIPLES

Data is valuable
- Data is an asset with unique properties
- The value of data can and should be expressed in economic terms
- Effective Data Management requires leadership commitment

Data Management requirements are business requirements
- Managing data means managing the quality of data
- It takes Metadata to manage data
- It takes planning to manage data
- Data Management requirements must drive Information Technology decisions

Data Management is lifecycle management	Data Management depends on diverse skills
• Different types of data have different lifecycle characteristics • Managing data includes managing the risks associated with data	• Data management is cross-functional • Data management requires an enterprise perspective • Data management must account for a range of perspectives

Figure 5: Data Management Principles (Adapted from DMBOK2, p. 22)

DATA MANAGEMENT PRINCIPLES AND DATA MANAGEMENT MATURITY

You now understand the importance of data management, the challenges of data management, and the principles of data management. Your organization is undoubtedly applying some of these principles, as it is undoubtedly following some of the practices that will be described in the upcoming chapters. But unless the organization raises its awareness through a level of self-assessment, it is unlikely to be able to improve its practices.

A capability maturity assessment is a very good means to this end. Capability Maturity Assessment is an approach to process improvement based on a framework – a Capability Maturity Model – that describes how characteristics of a process evolve from ad hoc to optimal.[11]

With each new level, process execution becomes more consistent, predictable, and reliable. Processes improve as they take on characteristics of the levels. Progression happens in a set order. No level can be skipped. Levels commonly include:

- Level 0 Absence of capability

- Level 1 Initial or Ad Hoc: Success depends on the competence of individuals

- Level 2 Repeatable: Minimum process discipline is in place

- Level 3 Defined: Standards are set and used

- Level 4 Managed: Processes are quantified and controlled

- Level 5 Optimized: Process improvement goals are quantified

Within each level, criteria are described across process features. For example, a maturity model may include criteria related to how processes are executed, including the level of automation of those processes. It may focus on policies and controls, as well as process details. Such an assessment helps identify what is working well, what is not working well, and where an organization has gaps.

---

[11] See Paulk, Mark C. "A history of the Capability Maturity Model for Software." https://bit.ly/2HTuIK6.

The maturation of the use of data management principles could progress as illustrated in Figure 6, where an organization moves from limited knowledge of data management principles to a state where the principles become drivers of organizational improvement.

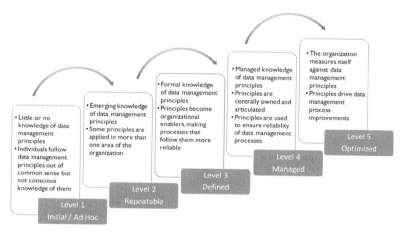

Figure 6: Maturity Model for the Application of Data Management Principles (adapted from DMBOK2, Chapter 15)

A Data Management Maturity Assessment (DMMA) can be used to evaluate data management overall, or it can be used to focus on a single functional or knowledge area, or even a single process or idea (such as the degree to which an organization follows data management principles).

Whatever the focus, a DMMA can help bridge the gap between business and IT perspectives on the health and effectiveness of data management practices. A DMMA provides a common language for depicting what progress looks like across data management functions and offers a stage-based path to improvement which can be tailored to an organization's strategic priorities. Thus, it can be used both to set and to measure organizational goals, as well as to compare one's organization against other organizations or industry benchmarks.

WHAT YOU NEED TO KNOW

- DAMA's data management principles were developed in response to the challenges presented by managing data.

- The principles enable an organization to take a more strategic approach to managing data.

- The principles can be used to formulate policy, define procedures, and enable strategic decisions.

- Staff involved with any aspect of data management should be familiar with these principles and be able to apply them to the work that they are accountable for.

- DAMA's data management principles can also be used in conjunction with a Data Management Maturity Assessment to understand the organization's current state and define a roadmap for improvement.

CHAPTER 4

Data Ethics

Defined simply, *ethics* are principles of behavior based on ideas of right and wrong. Ethical principles often focus on ideas such as fairness, respect, responsibility, integrity, justice, quality, reliability, transparency, and trust. Data handling ethics are concerned with how to procure, store, manage, use, and dispose of data in ways that are aligned with ethical principles. In other words, they are concerned with doing the right things with data and preventing the wrong things from being done with data, even when no one is looking.

Handling data – not only managing it, but using it and sharing it with other entities – in an ethical manner is necessary to the long-term success of any organization that wants to get value from its data. Unethical data handling can result in the loss of reputation and customers, because it puts at risk people whose data is exposed. In some cases, unethical practices are also illegal.[12] Given the connection between the right to privacy and

---

[12] HIPAA (Health Insurance Portability and Accountability Act) in the US, PIPEDA (Personal Information Protection and Electronic Documents Act) in Canada, the EU General Data Protection Regulation (GDPR) and other data protection /

other human rights, data ethics are also a matter of social responsibility.[13]

This chapter will discuss the importance of the ethical handling of data. It will cover:

- Why it is important to manage data ethically
- The principles underlying ethical data handling
- The benefits of taking an ethical approach to data management
- How to establish an ethical approach to data management

ETHICS AND DATA MANAGEMENT

The ethics of data handling center on several core concepts:

- **Impact on people**: Data often represents characteristics of individual people (customers, employees, patients, vendors, etc.) and is used to make decisions that affect people's lives. Ethics demands that data should be used only in ways that preserve human dignity.[14]

---

information privacy laws describe obligations toward the handling of personal identifying data (e.g., name, addresses, religious affiliation, or sexual orientation) and privacy (access or restriction to this information).

[13] The issue of data ethics has been examined not only in regard to privacy, but also in regard to the use of data to influence outcomes of political processes. See Nicholas Confessore and Danny Hakim, March 6, 2017. "Data Firm says 'Secret Sauce' Aided Trump; Many Scoff." *New York Times*. March 6, 2017. https://nyti.ms/2J2aDx2; and Barb Darrow, "Is Big Data Killing Democracy?" *Fortune Magazine*, September 15, 2017. Or, simply google: Is big data killing democracy?

[14] The accepted tenets of bioethics, which focus on preserving human dignity, provide a good general starting point for principles of data ethics. For example, the Belmont Principles for medical research may be adapted in Information

- **Potential for misuse**: Misusing data can negatively affect people and organizations. This leads to an ethical imperative to prevent the misuse of data, especially through actions that do harm to the greater good.

- **Economic value of data**: Data has economic value. Ethics of data ownership should determine how that value can be accessed and by whom.

Organizations protect data based largely on laws and regulatory requirements. Nevertheless, because data has an effect on people, data management professionals should recognize that there are ethical (as well as legal) reasons to protect data and ensure it is not misused. Even data that does not directly represent individuals, for example, data about the accessibility or distribution of resources, can still be used to make decisions that affect people's lives.

There is an ethical imperative not only to protect data, but also to manage its quality. People making decisions, as well as those impacted by decisions, expect data to be complete and accurate so that they have a sound basis for decisions. From both a business and a technical perspective, data management professionals have an ethical responsibility to manage data in a way that reduces the risk that it may misrepresent, be misused, or be misunderstood. This responsibility extends across the data lifecycle, from creation to destruction of data.

Unfortunately, many organizations fail to recognize and respond to the ethical obligations inherent in data management. They may adopt a traditional technical perspective and profess not to understand the data. Or they assume that if they follow the letter of the law, they have no risk related to data handling. This is a

---

Management disciplines (US-HSS, 1979). These principles include: respect for persons, the fundamental ethical requirement that people be treated in a way that respects their dignity and autonomy as human individuals; beneficence, the principle, first, to do no harm and, secondly, to maximize possible benefits and minimize possible harms; and justice, the principle to ensure fair and equitable treatment of people.

dangerous assumption. The data environment is evolving rapidly. Organizations are using data in ways they would not have imagined even a few years ago. Analytics can learn things from data that many people still would not think possible.[15]

While laws codify some ethical principles, legislation cannot keep up with the risks associated with evolution of the data environment. Organizations must recognize and respond to their ethical obligation to protect data entrusted to them by fostering and sustaining a culture that values the ethical handling of information.

ETHICAL PRINCIPLES UNDERLYING PRIVACY REGULATION

Public policy and law try to codify right and wrong based on ethical principles. But they cannot codify every circumstance. For example, privacy laws in the European Union, Canada, and the United States show different approaches to codifying data ethics. These principles can also provide a framework for organizational policy. The principles underlying the General Data Protection Regulation (GDPR) of the EU include:

- **Fairness, Lawfulness, Transparency**: Personal data shall be processed lawfully, fairly, and in a transparent manner in relation to the data subject.

---

[15] Numerous recent books describe the degree to which data science techniques have been used to influence political and economic processes in potentially unethical ways. See, for example, Stephens-Davidowitz, Seth. *Everybody Lies: Big Data, New Data, and What the Internet Can Tell Us About Who We Really Are*. (Harper Collins, 2017.) O'Neil, Cathy. *Weapons of Math Destruction: How Big Data Increases Inequality and Threatens Democracy*. (Random House, 2016.) And Schneier, Bruce. *Data and Goliath: The Hidden Battles to Collect Your Data and Control Your World*. (Norton, 2015.) The potential to misuse data has always existed. See Darell Huff's 1954 classic *How to Lie with Statistics*. But in today's world, the capacity to collect and analyze data has significantly increased the risk of misuse with significant social implications.

- **Purpose Limitation**: Personal data must be collected for specified, explicit, and legitimate purposes, and not processed in a manner that is incompatible with those purposes.

- **Data Minimization**: Personal data must be adequate, relevant, and limited to what is necessary in relation to the purposes for which they are processed.

- **Accuracy**: Personal data must be accurate, and where necessary, kept up-to-date. Every reasonable step must be taken to ensure that personal data that are inaccurate … are erased or rectified without delay.

- **Storage Limitation**: Data must be kept in a form that permits identification of data subjects [individuals] for no longer than is necessary for the purposes for which the personal data are processed.

- **Integrity and Confidentiality**: Data must be processed in a manner that ensures appropriate security of the personal data, including protection against unauthorized or unlawful processing and against accidental loss, destruction or damage, using appropriate technical or organizational measures.

- **Accountability**: Data Controllers shall be responsible for, and be able to demonstrate compliance with these principles.

GDPR principles are balanced by and support certain qualified rights individuals have to their data, including the rights to access, rectification of inaccurate data, portability, the right to object to processing of personal data that may cause damage or distress, and erasure. When personal data is processed based on consent, that consent must be an affirmative action that is freely given, specific, informed, and unambiguous. The GDPR requires effective governance and documentation to enable and demonstrate compliance and mandates Privacy by Design.

Canadian privacy law combines a comprehensive regime of privacy protection with industry self-regulation. PIPEDA (Personal Information Protection and Electronic Documents Act) applies to every organization that collects, uses, and disseminates personal information in the course of commercial activities. It stipulates rules, with exceptions, that organizations must follow in their use of consumers' personal information. Statutory obligations based on PIPEDA include:[16]

- **Accountability**: An organization is responsible for personal information under its control and must designate an individual to be accountable for the organization's compliance with the principle.

- **Identifying Purposes**: An organization must identify the purposes for which personal information is collected at or before the time the information is collected.

- **Consent**: An organization must obtain the knowledge and consent of the individual for the collection, use, or disclosure of personal information, except where inappropriate.

- **Limiting Collection, Use, Disclosure, and Retention**: The collection of personal information must be limited to that which is necessary for the purposes identified by the organization. Information shall be collected by fair and lawful means. Personal information shall not be used or disclosed for purposes other than those for which it was collected, except with the consent of the individual or as required by law. Personal information shall be retained only as long as necessary for the fulfillment of those purposes.

- **Accuracy**: Personal information must be as accurate, complete, and as up-to-date as is necessary for the purposes for which it is to be used.

---

[16] https://bit.ly/2tNM53c.

- **Safeguards**: Personal information must be protected by security safeguards appropriate to the sensitivity of the information.

- **Openness**: An organization must make specific information about its policies and practices relating to the management of their personal information readily available to individuals.

- **Individual Access**: Upon request, an individual shall be informed of the existence, use, and disclosure of his or her personal information, and shall be given access to that information. An individual shall be able to challenge the accuracy and completeness of the information and have it amended as appropriate.

- **Compliance Challenges**: An individual shall be able to address a challenge concerning compliance with the above principles to the designated individual or individuals accountable for the organization's compliance.

In March 2012, the US Federal Trade Commission (FTC) issued a report recommending organizations design and implement their own privacy programs based on best practices described in the report (i.e., Privacy by Design). The report reaffirms the FTC's focus on Fair Information Processing Principles, which include:

- **Notice / Awareness**: Data collectors must disclose their information practices before collecting personal information from consumers.

- **Choice / Consent**: Consumers must be given options with respect to whether and how personal information collected from them may be used for purposes beyond those for which the information was provided.

- **Access / Participation**: Consumers should be able to view and contest the accuracy and completeness of data collected about them.

- **Integrity / Security**: Data collectors must take reasonable steps to assure that information collected from consumers is accurate and secure from unauthorized use.

- **Enforcement / Redress**: The use of a reliable mechanism to impose sanctions for noncompliance with these fair information practices.

There is a global trend towards increasing legislative protection of individuals' information privacy, following the standards set by EU legislation. Laws around the world place different kinds of restrictions on the movement of data across international boundaries. Even within a multinational organization, there will be legal limits to sharing information globally. It is therefore important that organizations have policies and guidelines that enable staff to follow legal requirements as well as use data within the risk appetite of the organization.

ETHICS AND COMPETITIVE ADVANTAGE

Organizations are increasingly recognizing that an ethical approach to data use is a competitive business advantage.[17] Ethical data handling can increase the trustworthiness of an organization and the organization's data and process outcomes. This can create better relationships between the organization and its stakeholders. Creating an ethical culture entails introducing proper governance, including institution of controls to ensure that both intended and resulting outcomes of data processing are ethical and do not violate trust or infringe on human dignity.

Data handling doesn't happen in a vacuum. There are strong business reasons to handle data ethically:

- **Stakeholder expectations**: Customers and other stakeholders expect ethical behavior and outcomes from businesses and their data processes.

---

[17] Hasselbalch & Tranberg, 2016.

- **Managing risk**: Reducing the risk that data for which the organization is responsible will be misused by employees, customers, or partners is a primary reason to cultivate ethical principles for data handling.

- **Preventing misuse**: There is also an ethical responsibility to secure data from criminals (i.e., to protect against hacking and potential data beaches).

- **Respecting ownership**: Different models of data ownership influence the ethics of data handling. For example, technology has improved the ability of organizations to share data with each other. This ability means organizations need to make ethical decisions about their responsibility for sharing data that does not belong to them.

The emerging roles of Chief Data Officer, Chief Risk Officer, Chief Privacy Officer, and Chief Analytics Officer are focused on controlling risk by establishing acceptable practices for data handling. But responsibility extends beyond people in these roles. Handling data ethically requires organization-wide recognition of the risks associated with misuse of data, and organizational commitment to handling data based on principles that protect individuals and respect the imperatives related to data ownership.

Data governance can help ensure that ethical principles are followed for critical processes, such as deciding who can use data, as well as how they can use data. Data governance practitioners must consider the ethical risks of certain uses of data on stakeholders. They should manage these risks in a similar to how they manage data quality.

ESTABLISH A CULTURE OF ETHICAL DATA HANDLING

Establishing a culture of ethical data handling requires understanding existing practices, defining expected behaviors, codifying these in policies and a code of ethics, and providing training and oversight to enforce expected behaviors. As with other initiatives related to governing data and to changing culture, this process requires strong leadership.

Ethical handling of data obviously includes following the law. It also influences how data is analyzed, interpreted, and leveraged internally and externally. An organizational culture that values ethical behavior will not only have a code of conduct, it will also ensure that clear communication and governance controls are in place to support employees who become aware of unethical practices or risks. Employees need to be able to report such circumstances without fear of retaliation. Improving an organization's ethical behavior regarding data often requires a formal Organizational Change Management (OCM) process (see Chapter 12).

Steps to establishing a culture of ethical data handling include:

- **Review current state data handling practices**: Understand the degree to which current practices are directly and explicitly connected to ethical and compliance drivers; identify how well employees understand the ethical implications of existing practices in building and preserving the trust of customers, partners, and other stakeholders.

- **Identify principles, practices, and risk factors**: Understand the risk that data might be misused and cause harm to customers, employees, vendors, other stakeholders, or the organization as a whole. In addition to industry-related risks, most organizations have specific risks, which may be related to their technology footprint, their rate of employee turnover, the means by which they collect customer data, or other factors. Principles should be aligned with risks (bad things that can happen if the principles are not adhered to) and practices (the right ways of doing things so that risks are avoided). Practices should be supported by controls.

- **Adopt a socially responsible ethical risk model**: Executing business intelligence, analytics, and data science activities fairly requires an ethical perspective that looks beyond the boundaries of the organization and accounts for implications to the wider community. An ethical perspective is necessary not only because data can easily be misused but also because organizations have a social responsibility not to do harm with their data. A risk model can be used to determine whether to execute a project. It will also influence how to execute the project. Because data analytics projects are complex, people may not see the ethical challenges. Organizations need to actively identify potential risks. A risk model can help them do so (see Figure 7).

- **Create an ethical data handling strategy & roadmap**: After a review of current state and the development of a set of principles, an organization can formalize a strategy to improve its data handling practices. This strategy must express both ethical principles and expected behavior related to data, expressed in values statements and a code of ethical behavior.

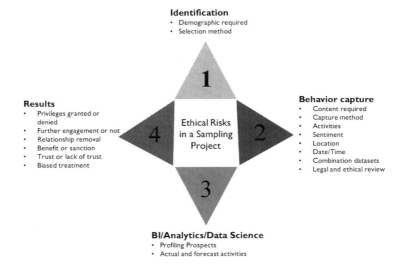

Identification
- Demographic required
- Selection method

Results
- Privileges granted or denied
- Further engagement or not
- Relationship removal
- Benefit or sanction
- Trust or lack of trust
- Biased treatment

1

Ethical Risks in a Sampling Project

4

2

Behavior capture
- Content required
- Capture method
- Activities
- Sentiment
- Location
- Date/Time
- Combination datasets
- Legal and ethical review

3

BI/Analytics/Data Science
- Profiling Prospects
- Actual and forecast activities

Figure 7: An Ethical Risk Model (DMBOK2, p. 64)

WHAT YOU NEED TO KNOW

- Organizations need to handle data ethically or they risk losing the good will of customers, employees, partners, and other stakeholders.

- Data ethics are grounded in fundamental principles and ethical imperatives.

- Data-related regulation is grounded in these same principles and imperatives, but regulation cannot cover every contingency. As such, organizations must account for the ethics of their own behavior.

- Organizations should cultivate a culture of ethical responsibility for the data they handle, not only to ensure they comply with regulations, but also because it is the right thing to do.

- Ultimately, ethical data handling provides a competitive advantage because it is the foundation for trust.

CHAPTER 5

Data Governance

Through an unfortunate accident of history, the term *data management* was originally used to describe the work that Database Administrators (DBAs) and other highly technical people did to ensure that data in large data banks was available and accessible. It is still strongly associated with those activities. The term *data governance* was introduced, in part, to make clear that managing data goes beyond managing databases. More importantly, data governance describes the processes by which organizations make decisions about data, decisions that need to be carried out by people throughout the enterprise.

In most enterprises data moves horizontally, across business verticals. If an organization is to leverage its data effectively across functions, it needs to establish common frameworks and policies to make consistent decisions about data across verticals. Data governance should play a role very similar to financial governance within an organization.

Data governance (DG) is defined as the exercise of authority and control (e.g., planning, monitoring, and enforcement) over the management of data assets. Governance activities help control data development and usage. They also reduce risks associated with data and enable an organization to leverage data strategically.

All organizations make decisions about data, regardless of whether they have a formal data governance function. Those that establish a formal data governance program exercise authority and control with greater intentionality and consistency.[18] Such organizations are better able to increase the value they get from their data assets.

This chapter will:

- Define data governance and discuss its importance
- Review different models for organizing data governance functions
- Discuss data governance activities, including data stewardship, and how they contribute to the organization

DATA GOVERNANCE AS OVERSIGHT

The data governance function guides all other data management functions. The purpose of data governance is to ensure that data is managed properly, according to policies and best practices.[19] A common analogy is to equate data governance to auditing and accounting. Auditors and controllers set the rules for managing financial assets. Data governance professionals set rules for managing data assets. Other areas carry out these rules. In either case, data governance is not a one-time thing; this oversight function must be sustained after it is established (see Figure 8). Principles for data governance need to be embedded in data management lifecycle and foundational activities (see Figure 1). An ongoing program, data governance requires ongoing commitment to ensuring that an organization gets value from its data and reduces risks related to data.

---

[18] Seiner, 2014.

[19] Ladley, 2012.

While the driver of data management overall is to ensure an organization gets value out of its data, data governance focuses on how decisions are made about data and how people and processes are expected to behave in relation to data. The scope and focus of a particular data governance program will depend on organizational needs. To achieve these goals, most data governance programs include:

- **Oversight**: Ensuring all data governance functional areas follow guiding principles for the sake of the enterprise.

- **Strategy**: Defining, communicating, and driving execution of data strategy and data governance strategy.

- **Policy**: Setting and enforcing policies related to data and Metadata management, access, usage, security, and quality.

- **Standards and quality**: Setting and enforcing data quality and data architecture standards.

- **Stewardship**: Providing hands-on observation, audit, and correction in key areas of quality, policy, and data management.

- **Compliance**: Ensuring the organization can meet data-related regulatory compliance requirements.

- **Issue management**: Identifying, defining, escalating, and resolving issues related to data security, data access, data quality, regulatory compliance, data ownership, policy, standards, terminology, or data governance procedures.

- **Data management projects**: Sponsoring efforts to improve data management practices.

- **Data asset valuation**: Setting standards and processes to consistently define the business value of data assets.

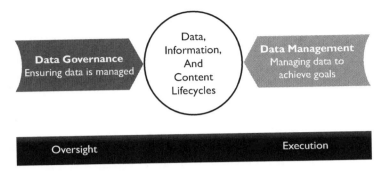

Figure 8: Data Governance / Data Management (DMBOK2, p. 72)

To accomplish these goals, a data governance program will articulate principles, develop policies and procedures, cultivate data stewardship practices at multiple levels within the organization, and engage in organizational change management efforts that actively communicate to the organization the benefits of improved data governance and the behaviors necessary to successfully manage data as an asset across the data lifecycle (see Figure 9).

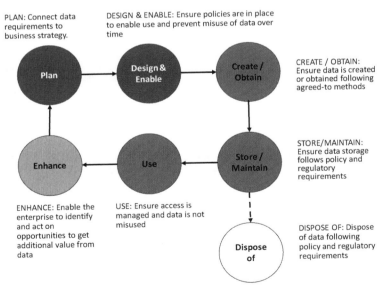

Figure 9: Data Governance and the Data Lifecycle (Adapted from DMBOK2, p. 29)

Many governance programs plan their roadmaps based on a capability maturity model that enables them to grow and improve their practices (see Chapter 3). For most organizations, adopting formal data governance requires the support of organizational change management, as well as sponsorship from a C-level executive, such as Chief Risk Officer, Chief Financial Officer, or Chief Data Officer.

BUSINESS DRIVERS FOR DATA GOVERNANCE

The most common driver for data governance is regulatory compliance, especially for heavily regulated industries, such as financial services and health care. Responding to evolving legislation requires strict data governance processes. The explosion in advanced analytics and data science has created an additional reason to implement governance structures.

While compliance or analytics may drive governance, many organizations back into data governance via an information management program driven by other business needs, such as Master Data Management (MDM), by major data problems, or both. A typical scenario: a company needs better customer data, it chooses to develop Customer MDM, and then it realizes that successful MDM requires data governance.

Data governance is not an end in itself. It needs to align directly with organizational strategy. The more clearly it helps solve organizational problems, the more likely people will be to change behaviors and adopt governance practices. Drivers for data governance most often focus on:

- **Reducing risks**, such as those related to compliance, the organization's general reputation, or to data security and privacy.

- **Improving processes**, such as the ability to comply with regulation, manage vendors, serve customers, and operate efficiently.

DATA GOVERNANCE PROGRAM CHARACTERISTICS

Ultimately, the goal of data governance, like the goal of data management generally is to enable an organization to manage data as an asset. Data governance provides the principles, policy, processes, framework, metrics, and oversight to manage data as an asset and to guide data management activities at all levels. To achieve this overall goal, a data governance program must be:

- **Sustainable**: Data governance is an ongoing process that requires organizational commitment. Data governance necessitates changes in how data is managed and used. This means managing change in a way that is sustainable beyond the initial implementation of any data governance component.

- **Embedded**: Data governance is not an add-on process. Data governance activities need to be incorporated into development methods for software, use of data for analytics, management of Master Data, and risk management.

- **Measured**: Data governance done well has positive financial impact, but demonstrating this impact requires understanding the starting point and planning for measurable improvement.

Implementing a data governance program requires commitment to change. The following principles, developed since the early 2000s, can help set a strong foundation for data governance:[20]

- **Leadership and strategy**: Successful data governance starts with visionary and committed leadership in support of enterprise business strategy.

- **Business-driven**: Data governance is a business program that must govern IT decisions related to data as much as it governs business interaction with data.

---

[20] The Data Governance Institute. https://bit.ly/1ef0tnb.

- **Shared responsibility**: Data governance is a shared responsibility between business data stewards and technical data management professionals.

- **Multi-layered**: Data governance occurs at both the enterprise and local levels, and often at levels in between.

- **Framework-based**: Because data governance activities require coordination across functional areas, the data governance program must establish an operating framework that defines accountabilities and interactions.

- **Principle-based**: Guiding principles are the foundation of data governance activities, and especially of data governance policy.

The core word in governance is *govern*. Data governance can be understood in terms of political governance. It includes:

- **Legislative-like functions:** Defining policies, standards, and the enterprise data architecture.

- **Judicial-like functions**: Issue management and escalation.

- **Executive functions**: Protecting and serving, administrative responsibilities.

To better manage risk, most organizations adopt a representative form of data governance, so that all stakeholders can be heard.

DATA GOVERNANCE MODELS

Each organization should adopt a governance model that supports its business strategy and is likely to succeed within its own cultural context. Models differ with respect to their organizational structure, level of formality, and approach to decision-making. Some models are centrally organized, while others are distributed. All models need a degree of flexibility. Organizations should also be prepared to evolve their model to meet new challenges and to be adaptive as organizational culture evolves.

Data governance organizations may also have multiple layers to address concerns at different levels within an enterprise – local, divisional, and enterprise-wide. The work of governance is often divided among multiple committees, each with a purpose and level of oversight different from the others. This work needs to be coordinated for an organization to benefit from synergy between the pieces.

Figure 10 represents a generic data governance model. The model involves activities at various levels within the organization (as noted on the vertical axis: local, divisional, enterprise), as well as separation of governance responsibilities within organizational functions and between business (left side) and technical/IT (right side).

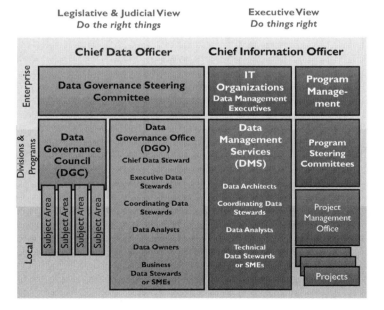

Figure 10: Data Governance Organization Components at Different Organizational Levels (DMBOK2, p. 74)

Much of the work of data governance is carried out at the ground level, by data stewards who are associated through a data governance office. Stewards may be full or part-time. They will be responsible for different types of data depending on the needs of the organization. Often they will lead subject area or function working groups that report up through a Data Governance Council. At the enterprise level on the business side, many organizations have a Data Governance Steering Committee at the executive level. The Steering Committee helps enforce directives across the enterprise and serves as an escalation point.

On the IT side, work is often split between programs with various projects, implemented through project teams, and operational responsibilities that are carried out by data management services or production support / operations teams. A level of stewardship is required on the IT side as well. Most organizations will need governance structures within both business and IT sides of the house, as well as an oversight function. The different parts of the organization charged with governance activities need to actively collaborate and coordinate. Figure 11 shows how this kind of model can be implemented in different various ways, depending on the organization's needs and constraints.

The organizational choices for data governance depend on the existing structure of the enterprise, the goals of data governance, and the organization's cultural disposition to centralization and collaboration. In a centralized model, one data governance organization oversees all activities in all subject areas. In a replicated model, the same DG operating model and standards are adopted by each business unit. In a federated model, one data governance organization coordinates with multiple business units to maintain consistent definitions and standards.

In addition to organizing people for data governance, it is also helpful to establish an operating model which defines the interaction between the governance organization and the people responsible for data management projects or initiatives, the engagement of change management activities to introduce this new program, and the model for issue management resolution pathways through governance. Figure 12 illustrates an example you can adapt to meet the requirements and match the culture of your organization. Regardless of your situation, several facets will remain the same. Executive functions provide oversight. The DGO works within domains. Policy is pushed down, and issues are escalated. Stewards and stakeholders engage at multiple levels.

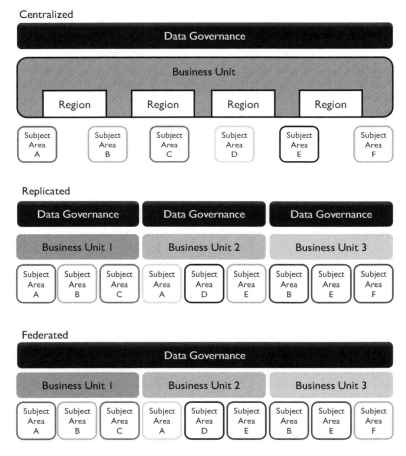

Figure 11: Enterprise Data Governance Operating Framework Examples (DMBOK2, p. 75)[21]

---

[21] Adapted from Ladley (2012).

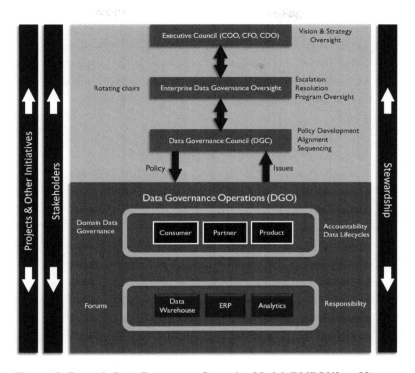

Figure 12: Example Data Governance Operating Model (DMBOK2, p. 83)

DATA STEWARDSHIP

Data Stewardship is one of those concepts that people don't always understand. A *steward* is a person whose job it is to manage the property of another person. Data Stewards manage data assets on behalf of others and in the best interests of the organization.[22] This concept grew out of the recognition that, within any organization, there have always been people who have expertise in the data and genuinely care about how an organization maintains data and makes it available for use. As the importance of data has grown, so too has formal recognition of this stewardship function.

---

[22] McGilvray, 2008.

Data Stewards represent the interests of all stakeholders and must take an enterprise perspective to ensure enterprise data is of high quality and can be used effectively. Effective Data Stewards are accountable and responsible for data governance activities and have a portion of their time dedicate to these activities. The term accounts for both informal stewards – those very helpful people in every organization who enable others to be successful. And formal stewards – those with "data steward" in their job titles.

The focus of stewardship activities will differ from organization to organization, depending on organizational strategy, culture, the problems an organization is trying to solve, its level of data management maturity, and the formality of its stewardship program. However, in most cases, data stewardship activities will focus on some, if not all, of the following:

- **Creating and managing core Metadata**:
  Standardization, definition and management of business terminology, valid data values, and other critical Metadata. Stewards are often responsible for an organization's Business Glossary, which becomes the system of record for business terms related to data.

- **Documenting rules and standards**:
  Definition/documentation of business rules, data standards, and data quality rules. Expectations used to define high-quality data are often formulated in terms of rules rooted in the business processes that create or consume data. Stewards help surface and refine these rules in order to ensure that there is consensus about them within the organization and that they are used consistently.

- **Managing data quality issues**: Stewards are often involved with the identification, prioritization, and resolution of data related issues or in facilitating the process of resolution.

- **Executing operational data governance activities**:
  Stewards are responsible for ensuring that data
  governance policies and initiatives are adhered to, from
  day to day and from one project to the next. They should
  influence decisions to ensure that data is managed in
  ways that support the overall goals of the organization.

LAUNCHING DATA GOVERNANCE

Data governance enables shared responsibility for data-related
decisions. Data governance activities cross organizational and
system boundaries in support of an integrated view of data.
Successful data governance requires a clear understanding of
what is being governed and who is being governed, as well as
who is governing.

Regardless of how they are organized, the data governance teams
perform similar activities. Before a program is set up, the data
governance team needs to understand the current state of the
organization's strategy, culture, and specific data challenges. The
goal of this assessment is to define what data governance means
to the organization and establish a data governance strategy.

Initial assessments are likely to include:

- **Data Management Maturity Assessment**: Determine
  how well the company uses people, processes, and
  technology to manage and get value from its data. This
  assessment can help determine levels of formal and
  informal stewardship, existing standards, etc. and
  identify opportunities for improvement.

- **Assessment of capacity to change**: Determine the
  capacity of the organization required to adopt behaviors
  required for successful data governance. Identify
  potential obstacles to a governance program.

- **Collaborative readiness**: Characterize the
  organization's ability to collaborate across functions to

steward and make consistent, holistic decisions about data.

- **Business alignment**: Assess how well the organization aligns its uses and management of data with business strategy. Identify critical organizational touch points for the data governance organization (e.g., procurement, budget/funding, regulatory compliance, SDLC standards).

- **Data quality assessment**: Identify critical data and existing data pain points in order to provide insight into existing issues and risks associated with data and business processes.

- **Regulatory compliance assessment**: Understand the relation of data risks to compliance requirements and how these are currently managed. Identify controls and monitoring that could improve the organization's ability to comply with regulations.

Initial assessments contribute to the business case for data governance. The maturity, data quality, and compliance assessments should identify concrete starting points for improvement, but the overall approach should be driven by a strategy that defines the scope and approach to data governance efforts in relation to business goals. The strategy should be defined through:

- A charter that defines goals and principles
- An operational framework with accountabilities
- An implementation roadmap and plan for operational success that describes:
    - o The target state of data governance activities and how they will be embedded in standard business and IT processes
    - o The initial set of initiatives to improve data management capabilities and data quality

- o The enterprise-wide benefits expected from the work
- o Metrics to demonstrate the benefits

Once the strategy is defined and the team begins work, they will execute the strategy by:

- Defining policies
- Underwriting data improvement projects
- Engaging with change management to educate staff and drive the adoption of desired behaviors
- Managing issues and conflicts that may arise during the process of implementation

SUSTAINABLE DATA GOVERNANCE

As described in the chapter introduction, the data governance function guides data management by establishing policies and best practices for managing data assets and by providing ongoing oversight of their implementation. Because these practices must be carried out by other areas, data governance principles must be embedded in data management lifecycle and foundational activities.

A successful data governance program will:

- Establish a strategy that aligns with and supports business strategy
- Define and enforce policies that define behaviors based on data management principles
- Set standards for data quality
- Provide stewardship of critical data
- Ensure the organization complies with data related regulations
- Manage issues related to aspects of data and governance itself

A successful DG program will also move the organization up the data management maturity curve by

- Sponsoring data management projects
- Standardizing data asset valuation
- Engaging in ongoing communication about the behaviors needed to get value from data

THE CHIEF DATA OFFICER

Most companies recognize at some level that data is a valuable corporate asset. In the last decade, some have appointed Chief Data Officers (CDO) to help bridge the gap between technology and business and evangelize an enterprise-wide data management strategy at a senior level. This role is on the rise. Forbes magazine reported in January 2018 that more than 60% of fortune 1000 firms have a CDO.[23]

While the requirements and functions of a CDO are specific to each company's culture, organizational structure, and business needs, many CDOs act as a combination of business strategist, adviser, data quality steward, and all-around data management ambassador.

In 2014, Dataversity published research outlining common mandates for a CDO.[24] These included:

- Establishing an organizational data strategy

- Aligning data-centric requirements with available IT and business resources

- Establishing data governance standards, policies and procedures

---

[23] See Randy Bean, "The Chief Data Officer Dilemna". Forbes.com, January 29, 2018. https://bit.ly/2J8ahVZ.

[24] Dataversity.com

- Providing advice (and perhaps services) to the business for data-dependent initiatives, such as business analytics, Big Data, data quality, and data technologies

- Evangelizing the importance of good information management principles to internal and external business stakeholders

- Providing oversight of data usage in analytics and business intelligence

Regardless of industry, it is common for a data management organization to report up through the CDO. In a more decentralized operating model, the CDO is responsible for the data strategy, but resources that are in IT, operations, or other lines of business execute that strategy. Some DMOs are established initially with the CDO just determining the strategy, and over time other aspects of data management, governance, and analytics are folded under the CDO umbrella as efficiencies and economies of scale are identified.

DATA GOVERNANCE AND LEADERSHIP COMMITMENT

More than any other aspect of data management, data governance requires leadership commitment and executive sponsorship. There are many potential obstacles to success. Governance focuses on getting people to behave differently toward data. Changing behaviors is challenging, especially for enterprise-wide initiatives. And governance of any kind can be perceived as an imposition, rather than as a means of improving processes and enabling success. But, if you educate yourself on the ways in which data supports your business strategy, you will quickly see and endorse the benefits of data governance:

- Making decisions about data in the context of overall business strategy makes more sense than making these decisions on a project-by-project basis

- Codifying expected behavior toward data in governance policies sets clear guidelines for employees and other stakeholders

- Defining data once and defining it consistently saves time, effort, and organizational churn

- Establishing and enforcing data standards is an efficient means of defining and then improving the quality of the organization's most critical data

- Reducing risks related to data privacy helps prevent data breaches and is good for an organization's reputation and bottom line

WHAT YOU NEED TO KNOW

- Data governance is an ongoing program that provides oversight for all other data management functions, by articulating strategy, establishing frameworks, setting policy, and enabling data usage across verticals.

- Data governance is not an end in itself. It is a means to achieve business goals.

- How the data governance function is organized depends on the goals of the data governance program and culture of the organization.

- DG helps organizations meet the challenges of data management by aligning activities and behaviors with principles of data management, along with guiding principles established to support an organization's business strategy.

- Data governance requires leadership commitment. That commitment will also enable other functions in data management functions to be more successful.

CHAPTER 6

Planning and Design in Data Lifecycle Management

Data Lifecycle management activities focus on planning and designing for data, enabling data use and maintenance, and actually using data to meet organizational goals (see Figure 1). Data architects and data modelers plan and design for data.

This chapter will describe:

- The role of enterprise architecture in planning and designing for the organization

- The critical function of data architecture within data management

- The goals and artifacts associated with data modeling

ENTERPRISE ARCHITECTURE

Architecture refers to an organized arrangement of component elements intended to optimize the function, performance, feasibility, cost, and aesthetics of an overall structure or system. The term *architecture* has been adopted to describe several facets of information systems design. Even in small organizations, information technology is complicated. Architectural artifacts and documentation which depict systems and data flows show people how systems, processes, and data work together. A strategic approach to architecture allows an organization to make better decisions about its systems and data.

Architecture practice is carried out at different levels within an organization (including enterprise, domain, or project) and with different areas of focus (e.g., infrastructure, application, or data). Table 1 describes and compares architectural domains. Architects from different domains must address development requirements collaboratively, as each domain influences the other domains.

A well-managed enterprise architecture practice can help an organization understand the current state of its systems, promote desirable change toward future state, enable regulatory compliance, and improve effectiveness. Effective management of data and the systems in which data is stored and used is a common goal of the breadth of architecture disciplines.

Type of Architecture	Purpose
Enterprise Business Architecture	To identify how an enterprise creates value for customers and other stakeholders
Enterprise Data Architecture	To describe how data should be organized and managed
Enterprise Applications Architecture	To describe the structure and functionality of applications in an enterprise
Enterprise Technology Architecture	To describe the physical technology needed to enable systems to function and deliver value

Type of Architecture	Elements
Enterprise Business Architecture	Business models, processes, capabilities, services, events, strategies, vocabulary
Enterprise Data Architecture	Data models, data definitions, data mapping specifications, data flows, structured data APIs
Enterprise Applications Architecture	Business systems, software packages, databases
Enterprise Technology Architecture	Technical platforms, networks, security, integration tools

Type of Architecture	Dependencies
Enterprise Business Architecture	Establishes requirements for the other domains
Enterprise Data Architecture	Manages data created and required by business architecture
Enterprise Applications Architecture	Acts on specified data according to business requirements
Enterprise Technology Architecture	Hosts and executes the application architecture

Type of Architecture	Roles
Enterprise Business Architecture	Business architects and analysts, business data stewards
Enterprise Data Architecture	Data architects and modelers, data stewards
Enterprise Applications Architecture	Application architects
Enterprise Technology Architecture	Infrastructure architects

Table 1: Architecture Domains (DMBOK2, p. 101-102)

THE ZACHMAN FRAMEWORK

An architecture framework is a foundational structure used to develop a broad range of related architectures. It provides a way of thinking about and understanding architecture and represents an overall 'architecture for architecture.' Exactly what architects do can be confusing to people who are not architects and who do not recognize the distinctions implied by these levels and focus areas. Architectural frameworks are valuable because they enable non-architects to understand the relationships (if not the detailed differences) between these concepts.

The most well-known enterprise architectural framework, the Zachman Framework, was developed by John A. Zachman in the 1980s. It has continued to evolve. Zachman recognized that in creating buildings, airplanes, enterprises, value chains, projects, or systems, there are many stakeholders, and each has a different perspective about architecture. He applied this concept to the requirements for different types and levels of architecture within an enterprise.

The Zachman Framework is represented by a 6x6 matrix that summarizes the complete set of models required to describe an enterprise and the relationships between them. It does not define how to create the models. It simply shows what models should exist (see Figure 13).

	What	How	Where	Who	When	Why	
Executive	Inventory Identification	Process Identification	Distribution Identification	Responsibility Identification	Timing Identification	Motivation Identification	Scope Context
Business Management	Inventory definition	Process Definition	Distribution Definition	Responsibility Definition	Timing Definition	Motivation Definition	Business Concepts
Architect	Inventory Representation	Process Representation	Distribution Representation	Responsibility Representation	Timing Representation	Motivation Representation	System Logic
Engineer	Inventory Specification	Process Specification	Distribution Specification	Responsibility Specification	Timing Specification	Motivation Specification	Technology Physics
Technician	Inventory Configuration	Process Configuration	Distribution Configuration	Responsibility Configuration	Timing Configuration	Motivation Configuration	Tool Components
Enterprise	Inventory Instantiations	Process Instantiations	Distribution Instantiations	Responsibility Instantiations	Timing Instantiations	Motivation Instantiations	Operational Instances
	Inventory Sets	Process Flows	Distribution Networks	Responsibility Assignments	Timing Cycles	Motivation Intentions	

Figure 13: Simplified Zachman Framework (DMBOK2, p. 103)

The Zachman framework summarizes the answers to a simple set of questions (i.e., what, how, where, who, when, why) that might be asked by stakeholders with different perspectives:

- **The executive perspective** (business context): Lists of business elements defining scope in *identification models*.

- **The business management perspective** (business concepts): Clarification of the relationships between business concepts defined by Executive Leaders as Owners in *definition models*.

- **The architect perspective** (business logic): System logical models detailing system requirements and unconstrained design represented by Architects as Designers in *representation models*.

- **The engineer perspective** (business physics): Physical models optimizing the design for implementation for specific use under the constraints of specific technology, people, costs, and timeframes specified by Engineers as Builders in *specification models*.

- **The technician perspective** (component assemblies): A technology-specific, out-of-context view of how components are assembled and operate configured by Technicians as Implementers in *configuration models*.

- **The user perspective** (operations classes): Actual functioning instances used by Workers as Participants. There are no models in this perspective.

The framework then identifies what kinds of architecture artifacts are required to answer these fundamental questions.

DATA ARCHITECTURE

Data architecture is fundamental to data management. Because most organizations have more data than individual people can comprehend, it is necessary to represent organizational data at different levels of abstraction so that management can understand it and make decisions about it.

The specialized discipline of data architecture can be understood from several perspectives:

- **Data architecture outcomes**, such as models, definitions and data flows on various levels (usually referred to as data architecture artifacts)

- **Data architecture activities**, to form, deploy and fulfill data architecture intentions

- **Data architecture behavior**, such as collaborations, mindsets, and skills among the various roles that affect the enterprise's data architecture

An organization's data architecture is described by an integrated collection of master design documents at different levels of abstraction, including standards that govern how data is collected, stored, arranged, used, and removed. It is also classified by descriptions of all the containers and paths that data takes through an organization's systems.

Data architecture artifacts include specifications used to describe existing state, define data requirements, guide data integration, and control data assets as put forth in a data strategy. The most detailed data architecture design document is a formal enterprise data model, containing data names, comprehensive data and Metadata definitions, conceptual and logical entities and relationships, and business rules. Physical data models are included, but as a product of data modeling and design, rather than data architecture.

Data architecture is most valuable when it fully supports the needs of the entire enterprise. Enterprise data architecture defines standard terms and designs for the elements that are important to the entire organization. The design of an enterprise data architecture includes depiction of the business data as such, including the collection, storage, integration, movement, and distribution of data. Enterprise data architecture enables consistent data standardization and integration across the enterprise.

Data architecture should serve as a bridge between business strategy and technology execution. As part of enterprise architecture, data architects:

- Strategically prepare organizations to quickly evolve their products, services, and data to take advantage of business opportunities inherent in emerging technologies

- Translate business needs into data and system requirements so that processes consistently have the data they require

- Manage complex data and information delivery throughout the enterprise

- Facilitate alignment between Business and IT

- Act as agents for change, transformation, and agility

These business drivers should influence measures of the value of data architecture.

DATA ARCHITECTURE ARTIFACTS

As data flows within an organization through feeds or interfaces, it is secured, integrated, stored, recorded, catalogued, shared, reported on, analyzed, and delivered to stakeholders. Along the way, the data may be verified, enhanced, linked, certified, aggregated, anonymized, and used for analytics until archived or purged. The enterprise data architecture descriptions must therefore include enterprise data models (e.g., data structures and data specifications), as well as data flow designs.

Data architects create and maintain organizational knowledge about data and the systems through which it moves. This knowledge enables an organization to manage its data as an asset and increase the value it gets from its data by identifying opportunities for data usage, cost reduction, and risk mitigation.

Architects seek to design in a way that brings value to the organization. This value comes through an optimal technical footprint, operational and project efficiencies, and the increased ability of the organization to use its data. To get there requires good design, planning, and the ability to ensure that the designs and plans are executed effectively.

ENTERPRISE DATA MODEL (EDM)

The EDM is a holistic, enterprise-level, implementation-independent conceptual or logical data model providing a common, consistent view of data across the enterprise. An EDM includes key enterprise data entities (i.e., business concepts), their relationships, critical guiding business rules, and some critical attributes. It sets forth the foundation for all data and data-related projects. Any project-level data model must be based on the EDM. The EDM should be reviewed by stakeholders, who should agree that it effectively represents the enterprise.

An organization that recognizes the need for an enterprise data model must decide how much time and effort it can devote to building it. EDMs can be built at different levels of detail, so resource availability will influence initial scope. Over time, as the needs of the enterprise demand, the scope and level of detail captured within an enterprise data model typically expands. Most successful enterprise data models are built incrementally and iteratively, using layers.

Figure 14 relates different types of models, and shows how conceptual models are ultimately linkable to physical application data models. It distinguishes:

- A conceptual overview over the enterprise's subject areas
- Views of entities and relationships for each subject area
- Detailed, partially attributed logical views of these same subject areas
- Logical and physical models specific to an application or project

All levels are part of the Enterprise Data Model, and linkages create paths to trace an entity from top to bottom and between models in the same level.

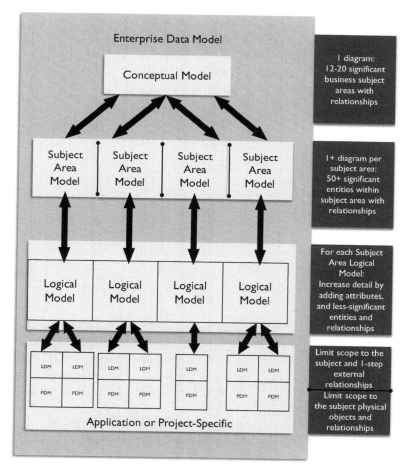

Figure 14: Enterprise Data Model (DMBOK2, p. 106)

DATA FLOW DESIGN

Data flow design defines the requirements and master blueprint for storage and processing across databases, applications, platforms, and networks (the components). These data flows map the movement of data to business processes, locations, business roles, and to technical components.

Data flows are a type of data lineage documentation that depicts how data moves through business processes and systems. End-to-end data flows illustrate where the data originated, where it is stored and used, and how it is transformed as it moves inside and between diverse processes and systems. Data lineage analysis can help explain the state of data at a given point in the data flow.

Data flows map and document relationships between data and

- Applications within a business process

- Data stores or databases in an environment

- Network segments (useful for security mapping)

- Business roles, depicting which roles have responsibility for creating, updating, using, and deleting data (CRUD)

- Locations where local differences occur

Data flows can be documented at different levels of detail: subject area, business entity, or even the attribute level. Systems can be represented by network segments, platforms, common application sets, or individual servers. Data flows can be represented by two-dimensional matrices (Figure 15) or in data flow diagrams (Figure 16).

The Enterprise Data Model and the Data Flow Design need to fit well together. As mentioned, both need to be reflected in current state and target state (architecture perspective), and also, the in transition state (project perspective).

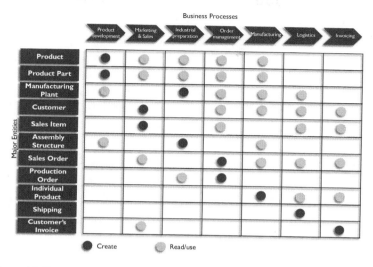

Figure 15: Data Flow depicted in a Two-Dimensional Matrix (DMBOK2, p. 108)

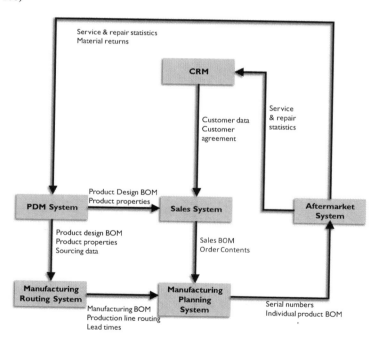

Figure 16: Data Flow Diagram Example (DMBOK2, p. 109)

DATA ARCHITECTURE AND DATA MANAGEMENT QUALITY AND INNOVATION

Data and enterprise architecture deal with complexity from two viewpoints:

- **Quality-oriented:** Focus on improving execution within business and IT development cycles. Unless architecture is managed, architecture will deteriorate. Systems will gradually become more complex and inflexible, creating risk for an organization. Uncontrolled data delivery, data copies, and interface 'spaghetti' relationships make organizations less efficient and reduce trust in the data.

- **Innovation-oriented:** Focus on transforming business and IT to address new expectations and opportunities. Driving innovation with disruptive technologies and data uses has become a role of the modern enterprise architect.

These two drivers require separate approaches.

- The quality-oriented approach aligns with traditional data architecture work where architectural quality improvements are accomplished incrementally through the architect's connection with projects. Typically, the architect keeps the entirety of architecture in mind and focuses on long-term goals directly connected to governance, standardization, and structured development.

- The innovation-oriented approach can have a shorter-term perspective and be using unproven business logic and leading edge technologies. This orientation often requires architects make contact with people within the organization with whom IT professionals do not usually interact; for example, product development representatives and business designers.

Working within enterprise architecture or as a data architecture team, data architects are responsible for developing a roadmap, managing enterprise data requirements within projects, and integrating with the overall enterprise architecture. Success depends on defining and adhering to standards and creating and maintaining useful and usable architectural artifacts. A disciplined architecture practice can improve efficiency and quality by creating reusable and extensible solutions.

DATA MODELING

A *model* is a representation of something that exists or a pattern for something to be made. Maps, organization charts, and building blueprints are examples of models in use every day. Model diagrams make use of standard symbols that allow one to understand content.

Data modeling is the process of discovering, analyzing, and scoping data requirements, and then representing and communicating these data requirements in a precise form called the *data model*. Data modeling is a critical component of data management. The modeling process requires that organizations discover and document how their data fits together.[25] Data models enable an organization to understand its data assets.

Data models comprise and contain Metadata essential to data consumers. Much of this Metadata uncovered during the data modeling process is essential to other data management functions. For example, definitions for data governance and lineage for data warehousing and analytics.

A data model describes an organization's data as the organization understands it or as the organization wants it to be. A data model contains a set of symbols with text labels that attempts visually to represent data requirements as communicated to the data modeler, for a specific set of data that can range in size from small (for a project) to large (for an organization).

---

[25] Simsion, 2007.

The model is thus a form of documentation for data requirements and data definitions resulting from the modeling process. Data models are the main medium used to communicate data requirements from business to IT, and within IT from analysts, modelers, and architects, to database designers and developers.

Data Models are critical to effective management of data because they:

- Provide a common vocabulary around data

- Capture and document explicit knowledge (Metadata) about an organization's data and systems

- Serve as a primary communications tool during projects

- Provide the starting point for customization, integration, or even replacement of an application

DATA MODELING GOALS

The goal of data modeling is to confirm and document understanding of different perspectives on data. This understanding leads to applications and data that more closely align with current and future business requirements. This understanding also creates a foundation to successfully complete broad-scoped initiatives such as Master Data Management and data governance programs. Proper data modeling leads to lower support costs and increases the reusability opportunities for future initiatives, thereby reducing the costs of building new applications. In addition, data models themselves are an important form of Metadata.

Confirming and documenting understanding of different perspectives facilitates:

- **Formalization**: A data model documents a concise definition of data structures and relationships. It enables assessment of how data is affected by implemented business rules, for current (as-is) states or desired target states. Formal definition imposes a disciplined structure to data that reduces the possibility of data anomalies occurring when accessing and persisting data. By illustrating the structures and relationships in the data, a data model makes data easier to consume.

- **Scope definition**: A data model can help explain the boundaries for data context and implementation of purchased application packages, projects, initiatives, or existing systems.

- **Knowledge retention/documentation**: A data model can preserve corporate memory regarding a system or project by capturing knowledge in an explicit form. It serves as documentation for future projects to use as the as-is version.

Data models help us understand an organization or business area, an existing application, or the impact of modifying an existing data structure. The data model becomes a reusable map to help business professionals, project managers, analysts, modelers, and developers understand data structure within the environment. In much the same way as the mapmaker learned and documented a geographic landscape for others to use for navigation, the modeler enables others to understand an information landscape.[26]

BUILDING BLOCKS OF DATA MODELS

There are many different kinds of data models, including relational, dimensional, etc. Modelers will use appropriate types of models based on the organization's needs, the data being modeled, and the system that the model is being developed for. Each type of model uses different visual conventions to capture information.

Models also differ based on the level of abstraction of the information they depict (conceptual with a high level of abstraction; logical with a medium level of abstraction; and physical which depicts a specific system or instantiation of data).

---

[26] Hoberman, 2009.

But models all use the same building blocks: entities, relationships, attributes, and domains.

As a leader in your organization, it is not necessary that you be able to read data models. However, it is helpful if you understand how they describe data. The definitions and examples here give you a flavor of how data models work.

Entity

Outside of data modeling, the definition of *entity* is a thing that exists separate from other things. Within data modeling, an entity is a thing about which an organization collects information. Entities are sometimes referred to as 'the nouns of an organization.' In relational data models, entities are the boxes that identify the concept being modeled.

An entity can be thought of as the answer to a fundamental question – who, what, when, where, why, or how – or to a combination of these questions. Table 2 defines and gives examples of commonly used entity categories.[27]

Relationship

A relationship is an association between entities.[28] A relationship captures the high-level interactions between conceptual entities, the detailed interactions between logical entities, and the constraints between physical entities. Relationships are shown as lines on the data modeling diagram.

In a relationship between two entities, *cardinality* captures how many of one entity (entity instances) participates in the relationship with how many of the other entity. For example, a Company can have one or many Employees.

---

[27] Hoberman, 2009.

[28] Chen, 76.

Category	Definition	Examples
Who	Person or organization of interest. That is, *Who* is important to the business? Often a 'who' is associated with a role such as Customer or Vendor. Persons or organizations can have multiple roles or be included in multiple parties.	Employee, Dependent, Patient, Player, Suspect, Customer, Vendor, Student, Passenger, Competitor, Author
What	Product or service of interest to the enterprise. It often refers to what the organization makes or what service it provides. That is, *What* is important to the business? Attributes for categories, types, etc. are very important here.	Product, Service, Raw Material, Finished Good, Course, Song, Photograph, Book
When	Calendar or time interval of interest to the enterprise. That is, *When* is the business in operation?	Time, Date, Month, Quarter, Year, Calendar, Semester, Fiscal Period, Minute, Departure Time
Where	Location of interest to the enterprise. Location can refer to actual places as well as electronic places. That is, *Where* is business conducted?	Mailing Address, Distribution Point, Web site URL, IP Address
Why	Event or transaction of interest to the enterprise. These events keep the business afloat. That is, *Why* is the business in business?	Order, Return, Complaint, Withdrawal, Deposit, Compliment, Inquiry, Trade, Claim
How	Documentation of the event of interest to the enterprise. Documents provide the evidence that the events occurred, such as a Purchase Order recording an Order event. That is, *How* do we know that an event occurred?	Invoice, Contract, Agreement, Account, Purchase Order, Speeding Ticket, Packing Slip, Trade Confirmation
Measure -ment	Counts, sums, etc. of the other categories (what, where) at or over points in time (when).	Sales, Item Count, Payments, Balance

Table 2: Commonly Used Entity Categories

Cardinality is represented by the symbols that appear on both ends of a relationship line. For cardinality, the choices are simple: zero, one, or many ("many" referring to any number higher than one). Each side of a relationship can have any combination of zero, one, or many.

Figure 17 shows different cardinality relationships. An Organization employs one or more Employees. An Employee can support zero, one, or many Dependents. But an Employee has one and only one Job during a time period. Cardinality relationships are a way of capturing rules and expectations related to data. If data shows that an Employee holds more than one Job during a set time period, then there is an error in the data, or the Organization is breaking a rule.

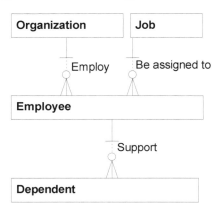

Figure 17: Relational Data Model with Cardinality

Attribute

An attribute is a property which identifies, describes, or measures an entity. The physical correspondent of an attribute in an entity is a column, field, tag, or node in a table, view, document, graph, or file. In the example in Figure 18, the entity Organization has the attributes of Organization Tax ID, Organization Phone Number, and Organization Name. Employee has the attributes of Employee Number, Employee First Name, Employee Last Name, and Employee Birth Date. Dependent and Job details have attributes that describe their characteristics.

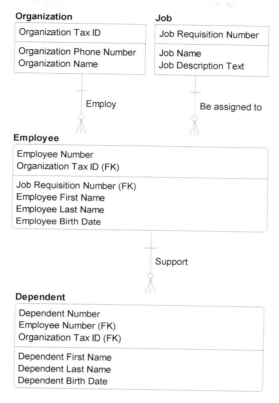

Figure 18: Relational Model with Attributes and Primary Keys

Domain

In data modeling, a domain is the complete set of possible values that an attribute can be assigned. A domain provides a means of standardizing the characteristics of the attributes and constrains the data that can be populated in the field. For example, the domain Date, which contains all possible valid dates, can be assigned to any date attribute in a logical data model or date columns/fields in a physical data model such as:

- EmployeeHireDate
- OrderEntryDate
- ClaimSubmitDate
- CourseStartDate

Domains are critical to understanding the quality of data. All values inside the domain are valid values. Those outside the domain are referred to as invalid values. An attribute should not contain values outside of its assigned domain. The domain for EmployeeHireDate may be defined simply as valid dates. Under this rule, the domain for EmployeeHireDate does not include February 30 of any year.

DATA MODELING AND DATA MANAGEMENT

Data Modeling is a process of discovering and documenting information that is critical to an organization's understanding of itself through its data. Models capture and enable use of knowledge within an organization. (That is, they are a critical form of and source of Metadata.) They can even be used to improve the quality of that information, through enforcement of naming conventions and other standards that make information more consistent and reliable.

Data analysts and designers act as intermediaries between information consumers (the people with business requirements for data) and the data producers who capture the data in usable form. Data professionals must balance the data requirements of the information consumers and the application requirements of data producers.

Data designers must also balance the short-term versus long-term business interests. Information consumers need data in a timely fashion to meet short-term business obligations and to take advantage of current business opportunities. System-development project teams must meet time and budget constraints. However, they must also meet the long-term interests of all stakeholders by ensuring that an organization's data resides in data structures that are secure, recoverable, sharable, and reusable, and that this data is as correct, timely, relevant, and usable as possible. Therefore, data models and database designs should provide a reasonable balance between the short-term and long-term needs of the enterprise.

WHAT YOU NEED TO KNOW

- Architecture is critical to an organization's ability to understand itself – its systems, its data, and the relationship between business and technical processes.

- A strategic approach to overall architecture enables an organization to make better decisions.

- Data architecture focuses on enabling an organization to understand and capture explicit knowledge about its own data.

- The Metadata created and managed through data architectural processes is critical to using and managing data over time.

- Data modeling is critical to data management because data models define entities that are important to the organization, concisely capture data requirements, and clarify rules and relationships that are necessary to manage data and the quality of data.

CHAPTER 7

Enabling and Maintaining Data

The focus of design work, such as data architecture and data modeling, is to provide insight on how best to set up applications that make usable, accessible, and current data available to the organization. Once data is set up in warehouses, marts, and applications, significant operational work is required to maintain data so that it continues to meet organizational requirements. This chapter will describe the data management functions that focus on enabling and maintaining data, including:

- Data Storage and Operations
- Data Integration and Interoperability
- Data Warehousing
- Reference Data Management
- Master Data Management
- Document and Content Management
- Big Data Storage

DATA STORAGE AND OPERATIONS

The data storage and operations function is what many people think about when they think about traditional data management. This is the highly technical work carried out by database administrators (DBAs) and network storage administrators (NSAs) to ensure that data storage systems are accessible and performant and that data integrity is maintained. The work of data storage and operations is essential to organizations that rely on data to transact their business.

Database administration is sometimes seen as a monolithic function, but DBAs play different roles. They may support production environments, development work, or specific applications and procedures. DBA work is influenced by the overall database architecture of an organization (e.g., centralized, distributed, federated; tightly or loosely coupled), as well as by how databases themselves are organized (hierarchically, relationally, or non-relationally). With the emergence of new technologies, DBAs and NSAs are responsible for creating and managing virtual environments (cloud computing). Because data storage environments are quite complex, DBAs look for ways to reduce or at least manage complexity through automation, reusability, and the application of standards and best practices.

While DBAs can seem far removed from the data governance function, their knowledge of the technical environment is essential to implement data governance directives related to such things as access control, data privacy, and data security. Experienced DBAs are also instrumental in enabling organizations to adopt and leverage new technologies.

Data storage and operations is about managing data across its lifecycle, from obtaining it to purging it. DBAs contribute to this process by:

- Defining storage requirements
- Defining access requirements
- Developing database instances
- Managing the physical storage environment

- Loading data
- Replicating data
- Tracking usage patterns
- Planning for business continuity
- Managing backup and recovery
- Managing database performance and availability
- Managing alternate environments (e.g., for development and test)
- Managing data migration
- Tracking data assets
- Enabling data audits and validation

In short, DBAs make sure the engines are running. They are also first on the scene when databases become unavailable.

DATA INTEGRATION AND INTEROPERABILITY

While data storage and operations activities focus on the environments for storing and maintaining data, data integration and interoperability (DII) activities include processes for moving and consolidating data within and between data stores and applications. Integration consolidates data into consistent forms, either physical or virtual. Data Interoperability is the ability for multiple systems to communicate. Data to be integrated usually originates from different systems within an organization. More and more, organizations also integrate external data with data they produce.

DII solutions enable basic data management functions on which most organizations depend:

- Data migration and conversion
- Data consolidation into hubs or marts
- Integration of vendor software packages into an organization's application portfolio
- Data sharing between applications and across organizations
- Distributing data across data stores and data centers

- Archiving data
- Managing data interfaces
- Obtaining and ingesting external data
- Integrating structured and unstructured data
- Providing operational intelligence and management decision support

The implementation of Data Integration & Interoperability practices and solutions aims to:

- Make data available in the format and timeframe needed by data consumers, both human and system
- Consolidate data physically and virtually into data hubs
- Lower the cost and complexity of managing solutions by developing shared models and interfaces
- Identify meaningful events (opportunities and threats) and automatically trigger alerts and actions
- Support Business Intelligence, analytics, Master Data Management, and operational efficiency efforts

The design of DII solutions needs to account for:

- **Change data capture**: How to ensure data is correctly updated

- **Latency**: The amount of time between when data is created or captured and when it is made available for consumption

- **Replication**: How data is distributed to ensure performance

- **Orchestration**: How different processes are organized and executed to preserve data consistency and continuity

The main driver for DII is to ensure that data moves efficiently to and from different data stores, both within the organization and between organizations. It is very important to design with an eye toward reducing complexity. Most enterprises have hundreds, sometimes thousands, of databases. If DII is not managed efficiently, just managing interfaces can overwhelm an IT organization.

Because of its complexity, DII is dependent on other areas of data management, including:

- **Data Governance**: For governing the transformation rules and message structures

- **Data Architecture**: For designing solutions

- **Data Security**: For ensuring solutions appropriately protect the security of data, whether it is persistent, virtual, or in motion between applications and organizations

- **Metadata**: For tracking the technical inventory of data (persistent, virtual, and in motion), the business meaning of the data, the business rules for transforming the data, and the operational history and lineage of the data

- **Data Storage and Operations**: For managing the physical instantiation of the solutions

- **Data Modeling and Design**: For designing the data structures including physical persistence in databases, virtual data structures, and messages passing information between applications and organizations

Data Integration & Interoperability is critical to Data Warehousing & Business Intelligence, as well as Reference Data and Master Data Management, because all of these transform and integrate data from multiple source systems to consolidated data hubs and from hubs to the target systems where it can be delivered to data consumers, both system and human.

Data Integration & Interoperability is central, as well, to the emerging area of Big Data management. Big Data seeks to integrate various types of data, including data structured and stored in databases, unstructured text data in documents or files, other types of unstructured data such as audio, video, and streaming data. This integrated data can be mined, used to develop predictive models, and deployed in operational intelligence activities.

When implementing DII, an organization should follow these principles:

- **Take an enterprise perspective** in design to ensure future extensibility, but implement through iterative and incremental delivery.

- **Balance local data needs with enterprise data needs**, including support and maintenance.

- **Ensure business accountability** for DII design and activity. Business experts should be involved in the design and modification of data transformation rules, both persistent and virtual.

DATA WAREHOUSING

Data warehouses allow organizations to integrate data from disparate systems into a common data model in order to support operational functions, compliance requirements, and Business Intelligence (BI) activities. Warehouse technology emerged in the 1980s and organizations began building warehouses in earnest in the 1990s. Warehouses promised to enable organizations to use their data more effectively by reducing data redundancy and bringing about more consistency.

The term *data warehouse* implies all the data is in one place, as in a physical warehouse. But data warehouses are more complicated than that. They consist of multiple parts through which data moves. During its movement, the structure and format of data may be changed, so that it can be brought together in common tables, from which it can be accessed. It may be used directly for reporting or as input for downstream applications.

Building a warehouse requires skills from across the spectrum of data management, from the highly technical skills required for data storage, operations, and integration, to the decision-making skills of data governance and data strategy leads. It also means managing the foundational processes that enable data to be secure, usable (via reliable Metadata), and of high-quality.

There are different ways to build a warehouse. The approach an organization takes will depend on its goals, strategy, and architecture. Whatever the approach, warehouses share common features:

- Warehouses store data from other systems and make it accessible and usable for analysis.

- The act of storage includes organizing the data in ways that increase its value. In many cases this means warehouses effectively create new data that is not available elsewhere.

- Organizations build warehouses because they need to make reliable, integrated data available to authorized stakeholders.

- Warehouse data serves many purposes, from support of work flow to operational management to predictive analytics.

The best known approaches to data warehousing have been driven by two influential thought leaders, Bill Inmon and Ralph Kimball.

Inmon defines a *data warehouse* as "a subject-oriented, integrated, time-variant and non-volatile collection of data in support of management's decision-making process"[29]. A normalized relational model is used to store and manage data. Figure 19 illustrates Inmon's approach, which is referred to as the "Corporate Information Factory."

---

[29]https://bit.ly/2J6ve3u.

Kimball defines a warehouse as "a copy of transaction data specifically structured for query and analysis." Figure 20 illustrates Kimball's approach, which calls for a dimensional model.

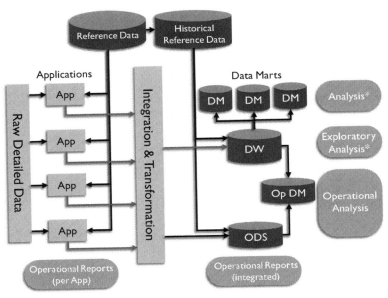

Figure 19: Inmon's Corporate Information Factory (DMBOK2, p. 388)[30]

As we approach the third decade of the new millennium, many organizations are building second- and third-generation warehouses or adopting data lakes to make data available. Data lakes make more data available at a higher velocity, creating the opportunity to move from retrospective analysis of business trends to predictive analytics.

---

[30] Adapted from figures in Inmon, W., Claudia Imhoff, and Ryan Sousa. *The Corporate Information Factory*. 2nd ed. Wiley 2001.

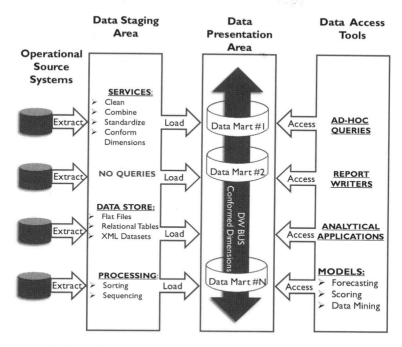

Figure 20: Kimball's Data Warehouse Chess Pieces (DMBOK2, p. 390)[31]

Managing bigger data takes additional knowledge and planning. But it also requires following some principles fundamental to managing warehouse data, including:

- **Focus on business goals**: Make sure data warehouse (DW) serves organizational priorities and solves business problems. Doing so requires a strategic perspective, which, most often, is an enterprise perspective.

- **Start with the end in mind**: DW content should be driven by the business priorities and the scope of end-data-delivery for BI.

---

[31] Adapted from figures in *The Data Warehouse Toolkit*, 2nd Edition, Ralph Kimball and Margy Ross, John Wiley & Sons, 2002.

- **Think and design globally; act and build locally**: Let end-vision guide the architecture, but build and deliver incrementally, through focused projects or sprints that enable more immediate return on investment.

- **Summarize and optimize last, not first**: Build on the atomic data. Aggregate and summarize to meet requirements and ensure performance, not to replace the detail.

- **Promote transparency and self-service**: The more context (e.g., including Metadata of multiple kinds) provided, the better able data consumers will be to get value out of the data. Keep stakeholders informed about the data and the processes by which it is integrated.

- **Build Metadata with the warehouse**: Critical to DW success is the ability to explain the data. For example, being able to answer basic questions like "Why is this sum X?" "How was that computed?" and "Where did the data come from?" Metadata should be captured as part of the development cycle and managed as part of ongoing operations.

- **Collaborate**: Collaborate with other data initiatives, especially those for data governance, data quality, and Metadata.

- **One size does not fit all**: Use the right tools and products for each group of data consumers.

REFERENCE DATA MANAGEMENT

Different types of data play different roles within an organization and have different data management requirements. Reference Data (for example, code and description tables) is data that is used solely to characterize other data in an organization, or solely to relate data in a database to information beyond the boundaries of the organization.[32]

Reference Data provides context critical to the creation and use of transactional and Master Data. It enables other data to be meaningfully understood. Importantly, it is a shared resource that should be managed at the enterprise level. Having multiple instances of the same Reference Data is inefficient and inevitably leads to inconsistency between them. Inconsistency leads to ambiguity, and ambiguity introduces risk to an organization.

Reference Data Management (RDM) entails control over defined domain values and their definitions. The goal of RDM is to ensure the organization has access to a complete set of accurate and current values for each concept represented.

Because it is a shared resource and crosses internal organizational boundaries, ownership and responsibility for Reference Data are challenging for some organizations. Some reference data originates outside of the organization, other Reference Data may be created and maintained within a department but have potential value elsewhere in an organization. Determining responsibility for obtaining data and applying updates is part of managing it. Lack of accountability introduces risk, as differences in Reference Data may cause misunderstanding of data context (for example, when two business units have different values to classify the same concept).

Reference data often seems simpler than other data because reference data sets are generally smaller than other kinds of data. They have fewer columns and fewer rows. Even a large reference data set, like the USPS ZIP code file, is small relative to the daily financial transactions of even a medium-sized retailer. Reference data is also generally less volatile than other forms of data. With a few notable exceptions (like currency exchange rate data), reference data changes infrequently.

---

[32] Chisholm, 2008.

The challenge with managing reference data comes with its usage. For Reference Data Management to be effective (values up-to-date and consistent across multiple applications and uses), it needs to be managed through technology that enables human and system data consumers to access it in a timely and efficient way across multiple platforms.

As with managing other forms of data, managing reference data requires planning and design. Architecture and reference data models must account for how reference data will be stored, maintained, and shared. Because it is a shared resource, it requires a high degree of stewardship. To get the most value from a centrally managed reference data system, an organization should establish governance policies that require use of that system and prevent people from maintaining their own copies of reference data sets. This may require a level of organizational change management activity, as it can be challenging to get people to give up their spreadsheets for the good of the enterprise.

MASTER DATA MANAGEMENT

Like Reference Data, Master Data is a shared resource. Master Data is data about the business entities (e.g., employees, customers, products, vendors, financial structures, assets, and locations) that provide context for business transactions and analysis. An entity is a real-world object (like a person, organization, place, or thing). Entities are represented by entity instances, in the form of data / records. Master Data should represent the authoritative, most accurate data available about key business entities. When well-managed, Master Data values are trusted and can be used with confidence.

Master Data Management (MDM) entails control over Master Data values and identifiers that enable consistent use, across systems, of the most accurate and timely data about essential business entities. The goals include ensuring availability of accurate, current values while reducing the risk of ambiguous identifiers.

Put more simply: when people think of high-quality data, they usually think of well-managed Master Data. For example, a record of a customer that is complete, accurate, current, and usable is considered "well-managed." From this record, they should be able to bring together an historical understanding of that customer. If they have enough information, they may be able to predict or influence the actions of that customer.

Master Data Management is challenging. It illustrates a fundamental challenge with data: people choose different ways to represent similar concepts and reconciliation between these representations is not always straightforward. As importantly, information changes over time and systematically accounting for these changes takes planning, data knowledge, and technical skills. In short, it takes work, including data stewardship and governance work, to manage Master Data.

Any organization that has recognized the need for MDM probably already has a complex system landscape, with multiple ways of capturing and storing references to real world entities. As a result of organic growth over time and from mergers and acquisitions, the systems that provided input to the MDM process may have different definitions of the entities themselves and very likely have different standards for data quality. Because of this complexity, it is best to approach Master Data Management one data domain at a time. Start small, with a handful of attributes, and build out over time.

Planning for Master Data Management includes several basic steps. Within a domain:

- Identify candidate sources that will provide a comprehensive view of the Master Data entities
- Develop rules for accurately matching and merging entity instances
- Establish an approach to identify and restore inappropriately matched and merged data
- Establish an approach to distribute trusted data to systems across the enterprise

Executing the process, though, is not as simple as these steps make it sound. MDM is a lifecycle management process. In addition, Master Data must not only be managed within an MDM system, it must also be made available for use by other systems and processes. This requires technology that enables sharing and feedback. It must also be backed up by policies that require systems and business processes to use the Master Data values and prevent them from creating their own "versions of the truth."

Still, Master Data Management has many benefits. Well-managed Master Data improves organizational efficiency and reduces the risks associated with differences in data structure across systems and processes. It also creates opportunity for enrichment of some categories of data. For example, customer and client data can be augmented with information from external sources, such as vendors that sell marketing or demographic data.

DOCUMENT AND CONTENT MANAGEMENT

Documents, records, and content (for example, the information stored on internet and intranet sites) comprise a form of data with distinct management requirements. Document and Content Management entails controlling the capture, storage, access, and use of data and information stored outside relational databases.[33] Like other types of data, documents and unstructured content are expected to be secure and of high quality. Ensuring their security and quality requires governance, reliable architecture, and well-managed Metadata.

Document and content management focuses on maintaining the integrity of and enabling access to documents and other unstructured or semi-structured information; this makes it

---

[33] The types of unstructured data have evolved since the early 2000s, as the capacity to capture and store digital information has grown. The concept of *unstructured data* continues to refer to data that is not pre-defined through a data model, whether relational or otherwise.

roughly equivalent to data operations management for relational databases. However, it also has strategic drivers. The primary business drivers for document and content management include regulatory compliance, the ability to respond to litigation and e-discovery requests, and business continuity requirements.

Document Management is the general term used to describe storage, inventory, and control of electronic and paper documents. It encompasses the techniques and technologies for controlling and organizing documents throughout their lifecycle.

Records Management is a specialized form of document management that focuses on records – documents that provide evidence of an organization's activities. These activities can be events, transactions, contracts, correspondence, policies, decisions, procedures, operations, personnel files, and financial statements. Records can be physical documents, electronic files and messages, or database contents.

Documents and other digital assets, such as videos, photographs, etc., contain content. *Content Management* refers to the processes, techniques, and technologies for organizing, categorizing, and structuring information resources so that they can be stored, published, and reused in multiple ways. Content may be volatile or static. It may be managed formally (strictly stored, managed, audited, retained or disposed of) or informally through ad hoc updates. Content management is particularly important in web sites and portals, but the techniques of indexing based on keywords and organizing based on taxonomies can be applied across technology platforms.

Successful management of documents, records, and other forms of shared content requires:

- Planning, including creating policies for different kinds of access and handling

- Defining information architecture and Metadata required to support a content strategy

- Enabling management of terminology, including ontologies and taxonomies, required to organize, store, and retrieve various forms of content

- Adopting technologies that enable management of the content lifecycle, from creating or capturing content to versioning, and ensuring content is secure

For records, retention and disposal policies are critical. Records must be kept for the required length of time, and they should be destroyed once their retention requirements are met. While they exist, records must be accessible to the appropriate people and processes and, like other content, they should be delivered through appropriate channels.

To accomplish these goals, organizations require content management systems (CMS), as well as tools to create and manage the Metadata that supports the use of content. They also require governance to oversee the policies and procedures that support content use and prevent misuse; this governance enables the organization to respond to litigation in a consistent and appropriate manner.

BIG DATA STORAGE

Big Data and data science are connected to significant technological changes that have allowed people to generate, store, and analyze larger and larger amounts of data and to use that data to predict and influence behavior, as well as to gain insight on a range of important subjects, such as health care practices, natural resource management, and economic development.

Early efforts to define the meaning of Big Data characterized it in terms of the Three V's: Volume, Velocity, Variety.[34] As more organizations start to leverage the potential of Big Data, the list of V's has expanded:

---

[34] Laney, 2001.

- **Volume:** Refers to the amount of data. Big Data often has thousands of entities or elements in billions of records.

- **Velocity:** Refers to the speed at which data is captured, generated, or shared. Big Data is often generated and can also be distributed and even analyzed in real-time.

- **Variety / Variability:** Refers to the forms in which data is captured or delivered. Big Data comes requires storage of multiple formats. Data structure is often inconsistent within or across data sets.

- **Viscosity:** Refers to how difficult the data is to use or integrate.

- **Volatility**: Refers to how often data changes and therefore how long the data is useful.

- **Veracity:** Refers to how trustworthy the data is.

Taking advantage of Big Data requires changes in technology and business processes and in the way that data is managed. Most data warehouses are based on relational models. Big Data is not generally organized in a relational model. Data warehousing depends on the concept of ETL (extract, transform, load). Big Data solutions, like data lakes, depend on the concept of ELT – loading and *then* transforming. This means much of the upfront work required for integration is not done for Big Data as it is for creating a data warehouse based on a data model. For some organizations and for some uses of data, this approach works, but for others, there is a need to focus on preparing data for use.

The speed and volume of data present challenges that require different approaches to critical aspects of data management, not only data integration, but also Metadata Management, and data quality assessment, and data storage (e.g., on site, in a data center, or in the cloud).

The promise of Big Data – that it will provide a different kind of insight – depends on being able to manage Big Data. In many ways, because of the wide variation in sources and formats, Big Data management requires more discipline than relational data management. Each of the V's presents the opportunity for chaos.

Principles related to Big Data management have yet to fully form, but one is very clear: organizations should carefully manage Metadata related to Big Data sources in order to have an accurate inventory of data files, their origins, and their value. Some people have questioned whether there is a need to manage the quality of Big Data, but the question itself reflects a lack of understanding of the definition of quality – fitness for purpose. Bigness, in and of itself, does not make data fit for purpose. Big Data also represents new ethical and security risks that need to be accounted for by data governance organizations (see Chapter 4).

Big Data can be used for a range of activities, from data mining to machine learning and predictive analytics. But to get there, an organization must have a starting point and a strategy. An organization's Big Data strategy needs to be aligned with and support its overall business strategy. It should evaluate:

- **What problems the organization is trying to solve. What it needs analytics for:** An organization may determine that the data is to be used to understand the business or the business environment; to prove ideas about the value of new products; to explore a hypothesis; or to invent a new way to do business. It is important to establish a gating and check point process to evaluate the value and feasibility of initiatives.

- **What data sources to use or acquire:** Internal sources may be easy to use, but may also be limited in scope. External sources may be useful, but are outside operational control (managed by others, or not controlled by anyone, as in the case of social media). Many vendors are competing as data brokers and often multiple sources exist for the desired data sets. Acquiring data that integrates with existing ingestion items can reduce overall investment costs.

- **The timeliness and scope of the data to provision:** Many elements can be provided in real-time feeds, snapshots at a point in time, or even integrated and summarized. Low latency data is ideal, but often comes at the expense of machine learning capabilities – there is a huge difference between computational algorithms directed to data-at-rest versus streaming. Do not minimize the level of integration required for downstream usage.

- **The impact on and relation to other data structures**: You may need to make changes to structure or content in other data structures to make them suitable for integration with Big Data sets.

- **Influences to existing modeled data**: Including extending the knowledge on customers, products, and marketing approaches.

The strategy will drive the scope and timing of organization's Big Data capability roadmap.

Many organizations are integrating Big Data into their overall data management environment (see Figure 21). Data moves from source systems into a staging area, where it may be cleansed and enriched. It is then integrated and stored in the data warehouse (DW) and/or an operational data store (ODS). From the DW, users may access data via marts or cubes, and utilize it for various kinds of reporting. Big Data goes through a similar process, but with a significant difference: while most warehouses integrate data before landing it in tables, Big Data solutions ingest data before integrating it. Big Data BI may include predictive analytics and data mining, as well as more traditional forms of reporting.

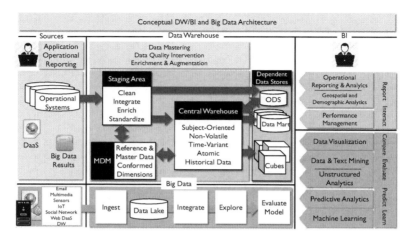

Figure 21: Conceptual DW/BI and Big Data Architecture (DMBOK2, p. 391)

WHAT YOU NEED TO KNOW

- The processes used to enable and maintain data are wide, varied, and constantly evolving.

- Different types of data have specific maintenance requirements, but for all types an organization must account for data volatility (the rate, timing and types of expected changes) as well as quality (fitness for purpose).

- Good planning and design can help reduce the complexity associated with these processes.

- Reliable and appropriate technology and disciplined execution of operational processes are critical to an organization's ability to manage its data.

- Even as data and technology evolve (e.g., from documents to Big Data), the same fundamental principles apply in managing it.

CHAPTER 8

Using and Enhancing Data

One characteristic of data that differentiates it from other assets is that it is not "consumed" when used. Different people and processes can even use the same data at the same time, or use the same data multiple times without depleting it.[35] Not only is data non-deplete-able, but many uses of data actually create more data. For example, aggregations and calculations of existing data sets create new data sets, as do predictive models created by data scientists. In many cases, these new data sets will continue to be produced and updated. They require management. They need to be defined and supported through Metadata. Expectations related to their quality must also be defined. Their access and use must be governed.

This chapter will look at activities within the data lifecycle where data is used and enhanced, including:

- Master Data Usage
- Business Intelligence
- Data Science

---

[35] Aiken & Billings, 2014.

- Analytics
- Data Visualization
- Data Monetization

MASTER DATA USAGE

The use of Master Data provides a good illustration of how using data is directly connected to enhancing data. Well-managed Master Data allows an organization to have a good understanding of the entities (customers, clients, vendors, products, etc.) with which it interacts and transacts business.

In the process of transacting business, an organization learns more about these entities – what they buy, what they sell, how best to contact them. What it learns may be stored at the level of the transaction, but organizations collect data that is necessary to maintain their Master Data (e.g., changes of address, updates to contact information, etc.). Transactional data also allows them to obtain additional data (e.g., customer or client preferences, buying patterns, and the like) that can enhance their Master Data. While the dynamic interaction between different uses of data should be accounted for when planning for overall data management, this is the particular focus of Master Data Management.

BUSINESS INTELLIGENCE

The development of Business Intelligence reporting is another activity where the use of data results in the creation of new data that requires a level of ongoing management.

The term *Business Intelligence* (BI) has two meanings.

- First, it refers to **a type of data analysis** aimed at understanding organizational activities and opportunities. When people say that data holds the key to competitive advantage, they are articulating the promise inherent in Business Intelligence activity: that if an organization asks the right questions of its own data, it can gain insights about its products, services, and customers that enable it to make better decisions about how to fulfill its strategic objectives.

- Secondly, *Business Intelligence* refers to **a set of technologies that support this kind of data analysis**. BI tools enable querying, data mining, statistical analysis, reporting, scenario modeling, data visualization, and dash-boarding. They are used for everything from budgeting to operational reporting and business performance metrics to advanced analytics.

BI is a primary driver for data warehousing, since traditional BI activities require reliable data sources that are integrated for usage. BI tools must support data exploration, as well as reporting. BI can evolve quickly as analysts use data. A successful program must have reliable foundational processes to:

- Maintain and enhance the core data used in BI reporting and enable incorporation of new data

- Maintain and enhance the BI tool set

- Manage Metadata related to BI reports, so that stakeholders understand the reports themselves

- Document the lineage of data in reports so that stakeholders know where the data came from

- Provide a data quality feedback loop, so that reports remain trustworthy and opportunities are identified to enhance them

In short, managing the data created by a BI program follows the lifecycle management steps that are part of overall data management.

DATA SCIENCE

Data science has existed for a long time. It used to be called applied statistics. But the capability to explore data patterns has quickly evolved in the twenty-first century with the advent of Big Data collection and storage technologies.

Data science merges data mining, statistical analysis, and machine learning with data integration and data modeling capabilities, to build predictive models that explore data content patterns. The term *data science* refers to the process of developing predictive models. The data analyst (or data scientist) uses the scientific method (observation, hypothesis, experimentation, analysis, and conclusion) to develop and assess an analytic or predictive model.

The data scientist develops a hypothesis about behavior that can be observed in the data prior to a particular action. For example, the purchase of one type of item is usually followed by the purchase of another type of item (the purchase of a house is usually followed by the purchase of furniture). Then, the data scientist analyzes large amounts of historical data to determine how frequently the hypothesis has been true in the past and to statistically verify the probable accuracy of the model.[36]

If a hypothesis is valid with sufficient frequency, and if the behavior it predicts is useful, then the model may become the basis for an operational intelligence process to predict future behavior, even possibly in real time such as suggestive selling advertisements.

In some ways, data science can be understood as an extension of BI. In other ways, however, it takes data analysis and use to a very different level. Traditional Business Intelligence provides 'rear-view mirror' reporting – analysis of structured data to

---

[36] Data Science models, which contain logic (algorithms) to process data and make predictions from it, are not the same thing as data models described in Chapter 6, which document the structure of data and the relationships between data entities and attributes.

describe past trends. In some cases, BI patterns are used to predict future behavior, but not with high confidence.

Until recently, in-depth analysis of enormous data sets has been limited by technology. Analyses have relied on sampling or other means of abstraction to approximate patterns. As the capacity to collect and analyze large data sets has grown, data scientists have integrated methods from mathematics, statistics, computer science, signal processing, probability modeling, pattern recognition, machine learning, uncertainty modeling, and data visualization in order to gain insight and predict behaviors based on Big Data sets. In short, data science has found new ways to analyze and extract knowledge from data. In many cases, this knowledge can be translated into economic value.

As Big Data has been brought into data warehousing and BI environments, data science techniques can provide a forward-looking ('windshield') view of the organization. Predictive capabilities, real-time and model-based, using different types of data sources, offer organizations better insight into where they are heading.

Data science models become sources of data. They need to be monitored and mined for insights. Like other forms of science, data science creates new knowledge and also new hypotheses. Testing hypotheses results in new models and new data. All of these pieces require management if they are to create value over time. Models need to be 'trained' and evaluated. New data sources can be incorporated into existing models. As with other data, the lifecycle of data to support data science efforts needs to be accounted for as part of planning and strategy.

PREDICTIVE AND PRESCRIPTIVE ANALYTICS

Much of data science is focused on the desire to create predictive models, though not all who create and use such models are data scientists. The simplest form of predictive model is the forecast. Predictive Analytics is the sub-field of supervised machine learning, rooted in statistics, where users attempt to model data elements and predict future outcomes through evaluation of probability estimates.

Predictive Analytics leverages probability models based on variables (including historical data) related to possible events (purchases, changes in price, etc.). When it receives other pieces of information, the model triggers a reaction by the organization. The triggering factor may be an event, such as a customer adding a product to an on-line shopping basket, or it may be data in a data stream, such as a news feed or utility sensor data, or an increased volume of service requests. The triggering factor may be an external event. News being reported about a company may serve as a predictor of a change in stock price. Predicting stock movement should include monitoring news and determining if news about a company is likely to be good or bad for the stock price.

Frequently, the triggering factor is the accumulation of a large volume of real-time data, such as an extremely high number of trades or requests for service or volatility of the environment. Monitoring a data event stream includes incrementally building on the populated models until a threshold is reached that activates the trigger.

The amount of time that a predictive model provides between the prediction and event predicted is frequently very small (in seconds or less). Investment in very low latency technology solutions, such as in-memory databases, high-speed networks, and even physically proximity to the source of the data, optimizes an organization's ability to react to the prediction.

Prescriptive analytics takes predictive analytics a step further to define actions that will affect outcomes, rather than just predicting the outcomes from actions that have occurred. Prescriptive analytics anticipates what will happen, when it will happen, and implies why it will happen. Because prescriptive analytics can show the implications of various decisions, it can suggest how to take advantage of an opportunity or avoid a risk. Prescriptive analytics can continually take in new data to re-predict and re-prescribe. This process can improve prediction accuracy and result in better prescriptions. Table 3 summarizes the relationship between traditional BI and data science.

Data Warehouse / Traditional BI	Data Science / Predictive Analytics	Data Science / Prescriptive Analytics
Hindsight	Insight	Foresight
Based on history: What happened? Why did it happen?	Based on predictive models: What is likely to happen?	Based on scenarios: What should we do to make things happen?
Descriptive	Predictive	Prescriptive

Table 3: Analytics Progression

DATA VISUALIZATION

Visualization is the process of interpreting concepts, ideas, and facts by using pictures or graphical representations. Data visualization facilitates understanding of the underlying data by summarizing it in a visual form, such as a chart or graph. Data visualizations condense and encapsulate characteristics data, making them easier to see. Doing so, they can surface opportunities, identify risks, or highlight messages.[37]

Visualization has long been critical to data analysis. Traditional BI tools include visualization options such as tables, pie charts, lines charts, area charts, bar charts, histograms, and turnkey boxes (also called candlesticks).

Figure 22, a control chart, represents a classic example of data visualization. It allows the viewer to quickly grasp how data has changed over time. Depending on what the chart reveals, an analyst might take a closer look at the details.

---

[37] Data visualization is an evolving field but the principles that guide it are based on design principles. See Tufte, (2001) and McCandless (2012). Numerous web-based resources exist with examples and counter examples. See the Periodic Table of Visualization Methods at Visual Literacy.Org https://bit.ly/IX1bvI.

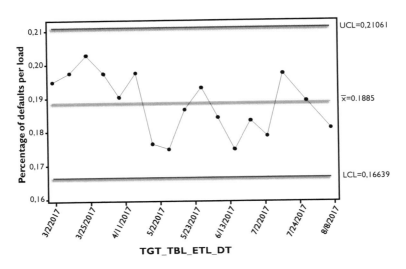

Figure 22: The Classic Control Chart (DMBOK2, p. 489)

Figure 23 shows a simple example of data visualization, a "Home Energy Report" presented by ENMAX, a utilities company based in Alberta, Canada, to its consumers. This infographic helps the consumers understand their home's energy use in relation to the population of similar homes and to the population of efficient homes. While this report doesn't talk about recommendations to save energy, it potentially helps the consumers ask relevant questions and set appropriate goals.[38]

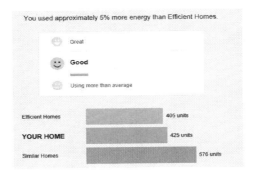

Figure 23: Home Energy Report of an ENMAX consumer

---

[38] *Data for Business Performance*, Southekal, Prashanth, Technics Publications, 2017.

The principles in these simple examples are extended significantly in data science applications. Data visualization is critical to data science because without it, interpretation of data is almost impossible. Patterns in a large data set can be difficult if not impossible to recognize in a numbers display. A pattern can be picked up fairly quickly when thousands of data points presented in a visual display.

Data visualizations can be delivered in a static format, such as a published report, or a more interactive online format. Some technologies for visualization enable analysts to move between layers of data, through filters or the ability to 'drill-in' to data. Others allow the visualization to be changed by the user on demand through innovative displays, such as data maps and moving landscapes of data over time.

To meet the growing need to understand data, the number of visualization tools has increased and techniques have improved. As data analytics matures, visualizing data in new ways will offer strategic advantages. Seeing new patterns in data can result in new business opportunities. As data visualization continues to evolve, organizations will have to grow their Business Intelligence teams to compete in an increasingly data-driven world. Business analytical departments will seek data experts with visualization skills (including data scientists, data artists, and data vision experts), in addition to traditional information architects and data modelers, especially given the risks associated with misleading visualization.

A critical success factor in implementing a data science approach is the alignment of the appropriate visualization tools to the user community. Depending on the size and nature of the organization, there are likely many different visualization tools being applied in a variety of processes. Ensure that users understand the relative complexity of the visualization tools. Sophisticated users will have increasingly complex demands. Coordination between enterprise architecture, portfolio management, and maintenance teams will be necessary to control visualization channels within and across the portfolio. Be aware that changing data providers or selection criteria will likely have downstream impacts to the elements available for visualization which can impact the effectiveness of tools.

It is a best practice to establish a community that defines and publishes visualization standards and guidelines and reviews artifacts within a specified delivery method; this is particularly vital for customer- and regulatory-facing content.

As do other uses of data, data visualization creates new data sets, in the form of the visualizations themselves, and in the methods by which data is combined so that it can be presented in a graphical format. You guessed it. This data must also be managed.

DATA MONETIZATION

Any organization engaged in Data Science or other forms of analytics is likely to gain valuable insight about its own customers, products, services, and processes. Advanced analytics can generate insight about external entities as well. Such an organization is also likely to develop techniques that might be valuable to others. If these insights and techniques can be packaged and sold, then an organization would be leveraging its data not only as an asset, but as a product. In some circles, direct data monetization is perceived as the holy grail of data management. Some companies (Dun & Bradstreet, Google, Amazon) have made a business of monetizing their data. But selling data and information is not the only way to get value from data assets.

In *Monetizing Data Management*, Peter Aiken and Juanita Billings point out that few organizations exploit the strategic advantage they may gain from data, "an organization's sole non-deplete-able, non-degrading, durable, strategic asset".[39] They make the case that improving data management practices is the first means of getting more value from data. An organization that

---

[39] Aiken and Billings, 2014.

puts a monetary value on effective data management practices will produce higher quality data and be able to do more with it.

Aiken and Billings assert that good data management practices are also the foundation for successful innovation of data uses. Poor data management practices, on the other hand, cost money and introduce risk to new initiatives and existing processes. The authors present case studies documenting that bad data management practices can result in direct waste through redundant work and, with it, the creation of redundant data, poor or missing Metadata, confusing processes, and incorrect information. They also provide examples of the benefits of disciplined data management practices. For example, clear and executable Metadata management practices increase organizational knowledge and make that knowledge transferrable.

Douglas Laney's *Infonomics,* a full-length study on managing information as an asset, presents a wide array of case studies demonstrating how organizations have leveraged their information assets to create value. While the industries, activities, and products differ, deriving economic value from data boils down to two basic methods:

- Exchanging information for goods, services, or cash

- Using information to increase revenue, reduce expenses, or manage risk

Laney presents 12 business drivers for monetizing data. One of the first ways is to get value is to use organizational data more effectively to retain existing customers, enter new markets, and create new products. But Laney goes beyond the obvious. For example, better data can improve organizational efficiency by enabling a company to reduce maintenance costs, negotiate for better terms and conditions, detect fraud and waste, or defray the costs of managing data.

Beyond being able to execute their operations, many organizations have barely scratched the surface of the promise of getting value from their data. For some, as Aiken and Billings's and Laney's case studies show and other research confirms, low quality data is a significant liability. Others, however, have been able to break through, with operational improvements as well as direct monetization. Case studies show that innovation uses of data require reliable data management. While not every organization will want to sell its data, all organizations want to have confidence in the decisions they make based on their data. The first step in this direction is to manage the data well.

WHAT YOU NEED TO KNOW

- When an organization uses data, it also creates new data that needs to be managed throughout its lifecycle. The requirements for lifecycle management are frequently missed in developing analytics.

- This new data is often the most valuable data an organization can possess because it is the source of insight.

- Due to evolving technologies and methods, this new data is may be created in ways that impact how data management requirements can be met.

- While new technologies offer innovative ways of working with data, they also exist alongside and interact with legacy data and legacy technology.

- Many organizations seek to get value from their data through monetization. A logical starting point is to improve data management practices. This work can both improve efficiency and create optimal conditions for direct monetization.

CHAPTER 9

Data Protection, Privacy, Security, and Risk Management

Managing data through its lifecycle depends on a set of foundational processes that enable the ongoing use and enhancement of data. These include protecting data from unauthorized use, managing Metadata (the knowledge required to understand and use data), and managing the quality of data. As noted earlier, foundational activities must be accounted for as part of planning and design and they must be carried out operationally. These activities are also supported by and integral to the success of governance structures (see Figure 1).

This chapter will discuss data protection and security. Data Security includes the planning, development, and execution of security policies and procedures to provide proper authentication, authorization, access, and auditing of data and information assets.

DATA SECURITY GOALS

The specifics of data security (which data needs to be protected, for example) differ between industries and countries. But the goal of data security practices is the same: to protect information assets in alignment with privacy and confidentiality regulations, contractual agreements, and business requirements. These requirements come from:

- **Stakeholders**: Organizations must recognize the privacy and confidentiality needs of their stakeholders, including clients, patients, students, citizens, suppliers, or business partners. Everyone in an organization must be a responsible trustee of data about stakeholders.

- **Government regulations**: Government regulations are in place to protect the interests of some stakeholders. Regulations have different goals. Some restrict access to information, while others ensure openness, transparency, and accountability. Regulations differ between countries, which means organizations that transact business internationally need to be aware of and able to meet data protection requirements where they do business.

- **Proprietary business concerns**: Each organization has proprietary data to protect. An organization's data provides insight into its customers and, when leveraged effectively, can provide a competitive advantage. If confidential data is stolen or breached, an organization can lose competitive advantage.

- **Legitimate access needs**: When securing data, organizations must also enable legitimate access. Business processes require individuals in certain roles be able to access, use, and maintain data.

- **Contractual obligations**: Contractual and non-disclosure agreements also influence data security requirements. For example, the PCI Standard, an agreement among credit card companies and individual business enterprises, demands that certain types of data be protected in defined ways (e.g., mandatory encryption for customer passwords).

Effective data security policies and procedures allow the right people to use and update data in the right way, and restrict all inappropriate access and updates (see Figure 24).[40]

Figure 24: Sources of Data Security Requirements (DMBOK p. 218)

Understanding and complying with the privacy and confidentiality interests and needs of all stakeholders is in the best interest of every organization. Client, supplier, and constituent relationships all trust in, and depend on, the responsible use of data.

The goals of data security activities include:

- Enabling appropriate access and preventing inappropriate access to enterprise data assets

---

[40] Ray, 2012.

- Enabling compliance with regulations and policies for privacy, protection, and confidentiality
- Ensuring that stakeholder requirements for privacy and confidentiality are met

DATA SECURITY PRINCIPLES

Because specific requirements change over time and differ between places, data security practices should follow guiding principles, including:

- **Collaboration**: Data Security is a collaborative effort involving IT security administrators, data stewards/data governance, internal and external audit teams, and the legal department.

- **Enterprise approach**: Data Security standards and policies must be applied consistently across the entire organization.

- **Proactive management**: Success in data security management depends on being proactive and dynamic, engaging all stakeholders, managing change, and overcoming organizational or cultural bottlenecks such as traditional separation of responsibilities between information security, information technology, data administration, and business stakeholders.

- **Clear accountability**: Roles and responsibilities must be clearly defined, including the 'chain of custody' for data across organizations and roles.

- **Metadata-driven**: Security classification for data elements is an essential part of data definition.

- **Reduce risk by reducing exposure**: Minimize sensitive/confidential data proliferation, especially to non-production environments.

Risk reduction and business growth are the primary drivers of data security activities. Ensuring that an organization's data is secure reduces risk and adds competitive advantage. Security itself is a valuable asset. There is also an ethical imperative to protect data (see Chapter 4).

Data security risks are associated with reputation, regulatory compliance, fiduciary responsibility for the enterprise and stockholders, and a legal and moral responsibility to protect the private and sensitive information of employees, business partners, and customers. Data breaches can cause a loss of reputation and customer confidence. Organizations can be fined for failure to comply with regulations and contractual obligations. Data security issues, breaches, and unwarranted restrictions on employee access to data can directly impact operational success.

Business growth includes attaining and sustaining operational business goals. Globally, electronic technology is pervasive in the office, marketplace, and home. Desktop and laptop computers, smart phones, tablets, and other devices are important elements of most business and government operations. The explosive growth of e-commerce has changed how organizations offer goods and services. In their personal lives, individuals have become accustomed to conducting business online with goods providers, medical agencies, utilities, governmental offices, and financial institutions. Trusted e-commerce drives profit and growth. Product and service quality relate to information security in a quite direct fashion: robust information security enables transactions and builds customer confidence.

The goals of mitigating risks and growing the business can be complementary and mutually supportive if they are integrated into a coherent strategy of information management and protection.

DATA SECURITY AND ENTERPRISE DATA MANAGEMENT

As data regulations increase — usually in response to data thefts and breaches — so do compliance requirements. Security organizations are often tasked with managing not only IT compliance requirements, but also policies, practices, data classifications, and access authorization rules across the organization.

As with other aspects of data management, it is best to address data security as an enterprise initiative, and to do so across the data lifecycle (see Figure 25). Without a coordinated effort, business units will find different solutions to security needs, increasing overall cost while potentially reducing security due to inconsistent protection. Ineffective security architecture or processes can cost organizations through breaches and lost productivity. An operational security strategy that is properly funded, systems-oriented, and consistent across the enterprise will reduce these risks.

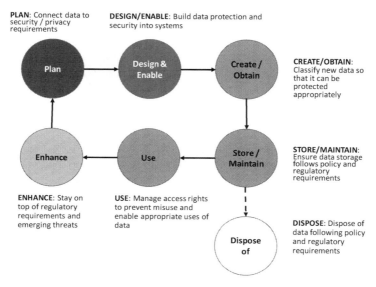

Figure 25: Data Security and the Data Lifecycle (Adapted from DMBOK2, p. 29)

Data and information security begin by assessing the current state of an organization's data in order to identify which data requires protection. The process includes the following steps:

- **Identify and classify sensitive data assets**: Depending on the industry and organization, there can be few or many assets, and a range of sensitive data – personal identification, medical, financial, etc.

- **Locate sensitive data throughout the enterprise**: Security requirements may differ, depending on where data is stored. A significant amount of sensitive data in a single location poses a high risk due to the damage possible from a single breach.

- **Determine how each asset needs to be protected**: The measures necessary to ensure security can vary between assets, depending on data content and the type of technology.

- **Identify how this information interacts with business processes**: Analysis of business processes is required to determine what access is allowed and under what conditions.

In addition to classifying the data itself, it is necessary to assess external threats, such as those from hackers and criminals, and internal risks posed by employees and processes. Much data is lost or exposed through the ignorance of employees who did not realize that the information was highly sensitive or who bypassed security policies. The customer sales data left on a web server that is hacked, the employee database downloaded onto a contractor's laptop that is subsequently stolen, and trade secrets left unencrypted in an executive's computer which goes missing, all result from missing or unenforced security controls.

The impact of security breaches on well-established brands in recent years has resulted in huge financial losses and a drop in customer trust. Not only are the external threats from the criminal hacking community becoming more sophisticated and targeted, the amount of damage done by external and internal threats, intentional or unintentional, has also been steadily increasing over the years.[41]

DATA SECURITY METADATA

One approach to managing sensitive data is via Metadata. Security classifications and regulatory sensitivity can be captured at the data element and data set level. Technology exists to tag data so that Metadata travel with the information as it flows across the enterprise. Developing a master repository of data characteristics means all parts of the enterprise can know precisely what level of protection sensitive information requires.

If a common standard is enforced, this approach enables multiple departments, business units, and vendors to use the same Metadata. Standard security Metadata can optimize data protection and guide business usage and technical support processes, leading to lower costs. This layer of information security can help prevent unauthorized access to and misuse of data assets.

When sensitive data is correctly identified as such, organizations build trust with their customers and partners. Security-related Metadata itself becomes a strategic asset, increasing the quality of transactions, reporting, and business analysis, while reducing the cost of protection and associated risks that lost or stolen information cause.

Data Classification is a prerequisite to managing data security. Two concepts drive security restrictions:

- **Confidentiality level:** *Confidential* means secret or private. Organizations determine which types of data should not be known outside the organization, or even within certain parts of the organization. Confidential information is shared only on a 'need-to-know' basis.

---

[41] Kark, 2009.

Levels of confidentiality depend on who needs to know certain kinds of information.

- **Regulatory categories**: These are assigned based on external rules, such as laws, treaties, customs agreements, and industry regulations. Regulatory information is shared on an 'allowed-to-know' basis. The ways in which data can be shared are governed by the details of the regulation.

The main difference between confidential and regulatory restrictions is where the restriction originates: confidentiality restrictions originate internally, while regulatory restrictions are externally-defined.

Another difference is that any data set, such as a document or a database view, can only have one confidentiality level. This level is established based on the most sensitive (and highest classified) item in the data set. Regulatory categorizations, however, are additive. A single data set may have data restricted based on multiple regulatory categories. To assure regulatory compliance, enforce all actions required for each category, along with the confidentiality requirements.

When applied to the user entitlement (the aggregation of the particular data elements to which a user authorization provides access), all protection policies must be followed, regardless of whether they originated internally or externally.

DATA SECURITY ARCHITECTURE

Enterprise architecture defines the information assets and components of an enterprise, their interrelationships, and business rules regarding transformation, principles, and guidelines. Data Security architecture is the component of enterprise architecture that describes how data security is implemented within the enterprise to satisfy the business rules and external regulations. Architecture influences:

- Tools used to manage data security
- Data encryption standards and mechanisms
- Access guidelines to external vendors and contractors
- Data transmission protocols over the internet
- Documentation requirements
- Remote access standards
- Security breach incident-reporting procedures

Security architecture is particularly important for the integration of data between:

- Internal systems and business units
- An organization and its external business partners
- An organization and regulatory agencies

For example, an architectural pattern of a service-oriented integration mechanism between internal and external parties would call for a data security implementation different from traditional electronic data interchange (EDI) integration architecture.

For a large enterprise, the formal liaison function between these disciplines is essential to protecting information from misuse, theft, exposure, and loss. Each party must be aware of elements that concern the others, so they can speak a common language and work toward shared goals.

PLANNING FOR DATA SECURITY

Planning for security includes process planning as well as data classification and architectural planning. It includes security not only of systems, but also of facilities, devices, and credentials. Implementing good practices starts with identifying requirements. These are based largely on regulations for particular industries and geographies. It is important to ensure an organization can meet requirements that may be driven by those with whom it interacts; for example, the European Union has stricter privacy requirements than does the United States.

Requirements will also be based on risks connected with the system landscape of the organization itself.

Requirements should be formalized into enterprise-wide policies and supported by clear standards for things like classification levels. Policies and standards need to be maintained as regulations evolve. Staff will require ongoing training, and data access and system usage will need to be monitored to ensure compliance.

Corporate culture deeply influences how we keep data secure. Organizations often end up reacting to crises, rather than proactively managing accountability and ensuring auditability. While perfect data security is next to impossible, the best way to avoid data security breaches is to build awareness and understanding of security requirements, policies, and procedures. Organizations can increase compliance through:

- **Training**: Promotion of standards through training on security initiatives at all levels of the organization. Follow training with evaluation mechanisms such as online tests focused on improving employee awareness. Such training and testing should be mandatory and a pre-requisite for employee performance evaluation.

- **Consistent policies**: Definition of data security policies and regulatory compliance policies for workgroups and departments that complement and align with enterprise policies. Adopting an 'act local' mindset helps engage people more actively.

- **Measure the benefits of security**: Link data security benefits to organizational initiatives. Organizations should include objective metrics for data security activities in their balanced scorecard measurements and project evaluations.

- **Set security requirements for vendors**: Include data security requirements in service level agreements and outsourcing contractual obligations. SLA agreements must include all data protection actions.

- **Build a sense of urgency**: Emphasize legal, contractual, and regulatory requirements to build a sense of urgency and an internal framework for data security management.

- **Ongoing communications**: Supporting a continual employee security-training program informing workers of safe computing practices and current threats. An ongoing program communicates that safe computing is important enough for management to support it.

WHAT YOU NEED TO KNOW

- Managing data security is foundational to data management success. Proper data protection is required to meet stakeholder expectations, and it is also the right thing to do for the enterprise.

- Data that is managed following data management best practices is also easier to protect, since it can be classified and tagged with a high degree of reliability.

- These practices include: taking an enterprise approach to security planning, establishing a reliable security architecture, and managing Metadata related to security.

- The necessity to protect data requires ensuring vendors and partners secure their data.

- Robust, demonstrable data security practices can become a differentiator, because they build trust.

CHAPTER 10

Metadata Management

Throughout this book, we have referred to the use and management of Metadata. One of the principles of data management is that Metadata is integral to managing data. In other words, you need data to manage data. Metadata describes what data you have. And if you don't know what data you have, you cannot manage it. Metadata management is a foundational activity that needs to be carried out throughout the data lifecycle. The lifecycle of Metadata also needs to be managed.

The most common definition of *Metadata,* "data about data," is misleadingly simple. For some it is, unfortunately, a source of confusion rather than clarification, because many kinds of information can be classified as Metadata, and there is not a clear line between "data" and "Metadata". Instead of trying to draw that line, we will describe how Metadata is used and why it is so important.

To understand Metadata's vital role in data management, imagine a large library, with hundreds of thousands of books and magazines, but no card catalog. Without a card catalog, readers might not even know how to start looking for a specific book or even a specific topic. The card catalog not only provides the necessary information (which books and materials the library owns and where they are shelved) it also enables patrons to find materials using different starting points (subject area, author, or title). Without the catalog, finding a specific book would be difficult if not impossible. An organization without Metadata is like a library without a card catalog.

Like other data, Metadata requires management. As the capacity of organizations to collect and store data increases, the role of Metadata in data management grows in importance. But Metadata management is not an end in itself; it is a means by which an organization can get more value from its data. To be data-driven, an organization must be Metadata-driven.

METADATA AND ITS BENEFITS

In data management, Metadata includes information about technical and business processes, data rules and constraints, and logical and physical data structures. It describes the data itself (e.g., databases, data elements, data models), the concepts the data represents (e.g., business processes, application systems, software code, technology infrastructure), and the connections (relationships) between the data and concepts. Metadata helps an organization understand its data, its systems, and its workflows. It enables data quality assessment and is integral to the management of databases and other applications. It contributes to the ability to process, maintain, integrate, secure, audit, and govern other data.

Data cannot be managed without Metadata. In addition, Metadata itself must be managed. Reliable, well-managed Metadata helps:

- Increase confidence in data by providing context, enabling consistent representation of the same concepts, and enabling the measurement of data quality

- Increase the value of strategic information (e.g., Master Data) by enabling multiple uses

- Improve operational efficiency by identifying redundant data and processes

- Prevent the use of out-of-date or incorrect data

- Protect sensitive information

- Reduce data-oriented research time

- Improve communication between data consumers and IT professionals

- Create accurate impact analysis thus reducing the risk of project failure

- Improve time-to-market by reducing system development lifecycle time

- Reduce training costs and lower the impact of staff turnover through thorough documentation of data context, history, and origin

- Support regulatory compliance

Organizations get more value out of their data assets if their data is of high quality. Quality data depends on governance. Because it explains the data and processes which enable organizations to function, Metadata is critical to data governance. If Metadata is a guide to the data in an organization, then it must be well-managed. Poorly managed Metadata leads to:

- Redundant data and data management processes

- Replicated and redundant dictionaries, repositories, and other Metadata storage

- Inconsistent definitions of data elements and risks associated with data misuse

- Competing and conflicting sources and versions of Metadata which reduce the confidence of data consumers

- Doubt about the reliability of Metadata and data

Well-executed Metadata management enables a consistent understanding of data resources and more efficient cross-organizational development.

TYPES OF METADATA

Metadata is generally categorized into three types: business, technical, or operational.

Business Metadata focuses largely on the content and condition of the data and also includes details related to data governance. Business Metadata includes the non-technical names and definitions of concepts, subject areas, entities, and attributes; attribute data types and other attribute properties; range descriptions; calculations; algorithms and business rules; valid domain values and their definitions. Examples of Business Metadata include:

- Data models, definitions and descriptions of data sets, tables, and columns

- Business rules, data quality rules, and transformation rules, calculations, and derivations

- Data provenance and data lineage

- Data standards and constraints

- Security/privacy level of data

- Known issues with data

- Data usage notes

Technical Metadata provides information about the technical details of data, the systems that store data, and the processes that move it within and between systems. Examples of Technical Metadata include:

- Physical database table and column names and properties

- Data access rights, groups, roles

- Data CRUD (create, replace, update and delete) rules

- ETL job details

- Data lineage documentation, including upstream and downstream change impact information

- Content update cycle job schedules and dependencies

Operational Metadata describes details of the processing and accessing of data. For example:

- Logs of job execution for batch programs

- Results of audit, balance, control measurements and error logs

- Reports and query access patterns, frequency, and execution time

- Patches and version maintenance plan and execution, current patching level

- Backup, retention, date created, disaster recovery provisions

These categories help people understand the range of information that falls under the umbrella of Metadata, as well as the functions that produce Metadata. However, the categories can also lead to confusion. People may be caught up in questions about which category a set of Metadata belongs to, or who is supposed to use it. It is best to think of these categories in relation to where Metadata originates, rather than how it is used. In relation to usage, the distinctions between Metadata types are not strict. Technical and operational staff use 'business' Metadata and vice versa.

METADATA IS DATA

While Metadata can be understood through its uses and the categories, it is important to remember that Metadata is data. Like other data, it has a lifecycle (see Figure 26). We must manage it in relation to its lifecycle.

An organization should plan for the Metadata it needs, design processes so that high-quality Metadata can be created and maintained, and augment its Metadata as it learns from its data.

METADATA AND DATA MANAGEMENT

Metadata is essential to data management as well as data usage. All large organizations produce and use a lot of data. Across an organization, different individuals will have different levels of data knowledge, but no individual will know everything about the data. This information must be documented or the organization risks losing valuable knowledge about itself. Metadata provides the primary means of capturing and managing organizational knowledge about data.

But Metadata management is not only a knowledge management challenge, it is also a risk management necessity. Metadata is necessary to ensure an organization can identify private or sensitive data and that it can manage the data lifecycle for its own benefit and in order to meet compliance requirements and minimize risk exposure.

Without reliable Metadata, an organization does not know what data it has, what the data represents, where it originates, how it moves through systems, who has access to it, or what it means for the data to be of high quality. Without Metadata, an organization cannot manage its data as an asset. Indeed, without Metadata, an organization may not be able to manage its data at all.

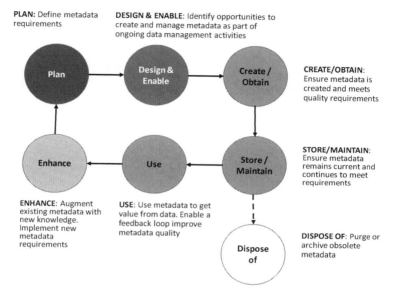

PLAN: Define metadata requirements

DESIGN & ENABLE: Identify opportunities to create and manage metadata as part of ongoing data management activities

CREATE/OBTAIN: Ensure metadata is created and meets quality requirements

STORE/MAINTAIN: Ensure metadata remains current and continues to meet requirements

ENHANCE: Augment existing metadata with new knowledge. Implement new metadata requirements

USE: Use metadata to get value from data. Enable a feedback loop improve metadata quality

DISPOSE OF: Purge or archive obsolete metadata

Figure 26: The Metadata Lifecycle (Adapted from DMBOK2, p. 29)

METADATA AND INTEROPERABILITY

As technology has evolved, the speed at which data is generated has also increased. Technical Metadata has become absolutely integral to the way in which data is moved and integrated. ISO's Metadata Registry Standard, ISO/IEC 11179, is intended to enable Metadata-driven exchange of data in a heterogeneous environment, based on exact definitions of data. Metadata present in XML and other formats enables use of the data. Other types of Metadata tagging allow data to be exchanged while retaining signifiers of ownership, security requirements, etc.

METADATA STRATEGY

As noted, the types of information that can be used as Metadata are wide-ranging. Metadata is created in various places throughout an enterprise. The challenges come with bringing Metadata together so that people and processes can use it.

A Metadata strategy describes how an organization intends to manage its Metadata and how it will move from current state to future state practices. A Metadata strategy should provide a framework for development teams to improve Metadata management. Developing Metadata requirements will help clarify the drivers of the strategy and identify potential obstacles to enacting it.

The strategy includes defining the organization's future state enterprise Metadata content and architecture and the implementation phases required to meet strategic objectives. Steps include:

- **Initiate Metadata strategy planning**: The goal of initiation and planning is to enable the Metadata strategy team to define its short- and long-term goals. Planning includes drafting a charter, scope, and objectives aligned with overall governance efforts and establishing a communications plan to support the effort. Key stakeholders should be involved in planning.

- **Conduct key stakeholder interviews**: Interviews with business and technical stakeholder provide a foundation of knowledge for the Metadata strategy.

- **Assess existing Metadata sources and information architecture**: Assessment determines the relative degree of difficulty in solving the Metadata and systems issues identified in the interviews and documentation review. During this stage, conduct detailed interviews of key IT staff and review documentation of the system architectures, data models, etc.

- **Develop future Metadata architecture**: Refine and confirm the future vision, and develop the long-term target architecture for the managed Metadata environment in this stage. This phase must account for strategic components, such as organization structure, alignment with data governance and stewardship, managed Metadata architecture, Metadata delivery architecture, technical architecture, and security architecture.

- **Develop a phased implementation plan**: Validate, integrate, and prioritize findings from the interviews and data analyses. Document the Metadata strategy and define a phased implementation approach to move from the existing to the future managed Metadata environment.

The strategy will evolve over time, as Metadata requirements, the architecture, and the lifecycle of Metadata are better understood.

UNDERSTAND METADATA REQUIREMENTS

Metadata requirements start with content: what Metadata is needed and at what level. For example, physical and logical names need to be captured for both columns and tables. Metadata content is wide-ranging and requirements will come from both business and technical data consumers.

There are also many functionality-focused requirements associated with a comprehensive Metadata solution:

- How frequently Metadata attributes and sets will be updated

- Timing of updates in relation to source changes

- Whether historical versions of Metadata need to be retained

- Who can access Metadata

- How users access (specific user interface functionality for access)

- How Metadata will be modeled for storage

- The degree of integration of Metadata from different sources; rules for integration

- Processes and rules for updating Metadata (logging and referring for approval)

- Roles and responsibilities for managing Metadata

- Metadata quality requirements

- Security for Metadata – some Metadata cannot be exposed because it will reveal the existence of highly protected data)

METADATA ARCHITECTURE

Like other forms of data, Metadata has a lifecycle. While there are different ways to architect a Metadata solution, conceptually, all Metadata management solutions include architectural layers that correspond to points in the Metadata lifecycle

- Metadata creation and sourcing
- Metadata storage in one or more repositories
- Metadata integration
- Metadata delivery
- Metadata access and usage
- Metadata control and management

A Metadata Management system must be capable of bringing together Metadata from many different sources. Systems will differ depending on the degree of integration and the role of the integrating system in the maintenance of the Metadata.

A managed Metadata environment should isolate the end user from the various and disparate Metadata sources. The architecture should provide a single access point for required Metadata. Design of the architecture depends on the specific requirements of the organization. Three technical architectural approaches to building a common Metadata repository mirror the approaches to designing data warehouses:

- **Centralized**: A centralized architecture consists of a single Metadata repository that contains copies of Metadata from the various sources. Organizations with limited IT resources, or those seeking to automate as much as possible, may choose to avoid this architecture option. Organizations seeking a high degree of consistency within the common Metadata repository can benefit from a centralized architecture.

- **Distributed**: A completely distributed architecture maintains a single access point. The Metadata retrieval engine responds to user requests by retrieving data from source systems in real time; there is no persistent repository. In this architecture, the Metadata management environment maintains the necessary source system catalogs and lookup information needed to process user queries and searches effectively. A common object request broker or similar middleware protocol accesses these source systems.

- **Hybrid**: A hybrid architecture combines characteristics of centralized and distributed architectures. Metadata still moves directly from the source systems into a centralized repository. However, the repository design only accounts for the user-added Metadata, the critical standardized items, and the additions from manual sources.

Implement a managed Metadata environment incrementally to minimize risks and facilitate acceptance. The repository contents should be generic in design. It should not merely reflect the source system database designs. Enterprise subject area experts should help create a comprehensive Metadata model for content. Planning should account for integrating Metadata so that data consumers can see across different data sources. The ability to do so will be one of the most valuable capabilities of the repository. It should house current, planned, and historical versions of the Metadata. Often, the first implementation is a pilot to prove concepts and learn about managing the Metadata environment.

METADATA QUALITY

When managing the quality of Metadata, it is important to recognize that a lot of Metadata originates through existing processes. For example, the data modeling process produces table and column definitions and other Metadata essential to creating data models. To get high-quality Metadata, Metadata should be seen as a product of these processes, rather than as a byproduct of them.

Again, Metadata follows the data lifecycle (see Figure 26). Reliable Metadata starts with a plan and increases in value as it is used, maintained, and enhanced. Metadata sources, like the data model, source to target mapping documentation, ETL logs, and the like should be treated as *data* sources. They should put in place processes and controls to ensure they produce a reliable, usable data product.

All processes, systems, and data have a need for some level of meta-information; that is, some description of their component pieces and how they work. It is best to plan how to create or collect this information. In addition, as the process, system or data is used, this meta-information grows and changes. It needs to be maintained and enhanced. Use of Metadata often results in recognition of requirements for additional Metadata. For example, sales people using customer data from two different systems may need to know where the data originated in order to better understand their customers.

Several general principles of Metadata management describe the means to manage Metadata for quality:

- **Accountability**: Recognize that Metadata is often produced through existing processes (data modeling, SDLC, business process definition) and hold process owners accountable for the quality of Metadata (both in its initial creation and its maintenance).

- **Standards**: Set, enforce, and audit standards for Metadata to simplify integration and enable use.

- **Improvement**: Create a feedback mechanism so that consumers can inform the Metadata Management team of Metadata that is incorrect or out-of-date.

Like other data, Metadata can be profiled and inspected for quality. Its maintenance should be scheduled or completed as an auditable part of project work.

METADATA GOVERNANCE

Moving from an unmanaged to a managed Metadata environment takes work and discipline. It is not easy to do, even if most people recognize the value of reliable Metadata. Organizational readiness is a major concern, as are methods for governance and control. A comprehensive Metadata approach requires that business and technology staff be able to work closely together in a cross-functional manner.

Metadata Management is a low priority in many organizations. An essential set of Metadata needs coordination and commitment in an organization. From a data management perspective, essential business Metadata includes data definitions, models, and architecture. Essential technical Metadata includes file and data set technical descriptions, job names, processing schedules, etc.

Organizations should determine their specific requirements for the management of the lifecycle of critical Metadata and establish governance processes to enable those requirements. It is recommended that formal roles and responsibilities be assigned to dedicated resources, especially in large or business critical areas. Metadata governance requires Metadata and controls, so the team charged with managing Metadata can test principles on the Metadata they create and use.

WHAT YOU NEED TO KNOW

- Metadata management is foundational to data management. You cannot manage data without Metadata.

- Metadata is not an end in itself. It is a means by which an organization captures explicit knowledge about its data in order to minimize risk and enable value.

- Most organizations do not manage their Metadata well and they pay the price in hidden costs; they increase the long-term cost of managing data by creating unnecessary rework (and with it, the risk of inconsistency) with each new project, as well as the operational costs of trying to locate and use data.

- Metadata is data. It has a lifecycle and should be managed based on that lifecycle. Different types of Metadata will have different specific lifecycle requirements.

- As the volume and velocity of data increase, the benefits of having reliable Metadata also increase.

CHAPTER 11

Data Quality Management

Effective data management involves a set of interrelated processes that enable an organization to use its data to achieve strategic goals. Data management includes the ability to design data for applications, store and access it securely, share it appropriately, and learn from it to meet strategic and operational objectives. Organizations that are trying to get value from their data need to know that their data is reliable and trustworthy. In other words, that their data is of high quality. But many factors can undermine data quality:

- Lack of understanding about the effects of poor quality data on organizational success
- Bad or insufficient planning
- Isolated design of processes and systems ('silos')
- Inconsistent technical development processes
- Incomplete documentation and Metadata
- Lack of standards and governance

Many organizations simply fail to define what makes data fit for purpose in the first place and therefore lack commitment to data quality.

All data management disciplines contribute to the quality of data, and high-quality data that supports the organization should be the goal of all data management disciplines. Because uninformed decisions or actions by anyone who interacts with data can result in poor quality data, producing high-quality data requires cross-functional commitment and coordination. Organizations and teams should be aware of this and should plan for high-quality data, by executing processes and projects in ways that account for the risks related to unexpected or unacceptable conditions in the data.

Because no organization has perfect business processes, perfect technical processes, or perfect data management practices, all organizations experience problems related to the quality of their data. These problems can be very costly. Organizations that formally manage the quality of data have fewer problems than those that leave data quality to chance.

Data quality is becoming a business necessity. The ability to demonstrate that data is of high quality, like the ability to demonstrate that data has been protected properly, is required by some regulations. Business partners and customers expect data to be reliable. An organization that can show that it manages its data well gains a competitive advantage.

This chapter will define key concepts related to data quality and discuss data quality management in relation to overall data management.

DATA QUALITY

The term *data quality* is used to refer both to the characteristics associated with high-quality data and to the processes used to measure or improve the quality of data. This dual usage can be confusing, so it helps to look at both meanings, starting with *high-quality data*. Later in the chapter we will look at the definition of *data quality management*.

Data is of high quality to the degree that it meets the expectations and needs of data consumers. That is, if the data is fit for the purposes of data consumers. It is of low quality if it is not fit for those purposes. Data quality is thus dependent on context and on the needs of the data consumers.

One of the challenges in managing the quality of data is that expectations related to quality are not always known. Customers may not articulate them. Often, the people managing data do not even ask about these requirements. But if data is to be reliable and trustworthy, then data management professionals need to better understand the quality requirements of their customers and how to measure them and meet them. The conversation about expectations needs to be ongoing, because requirements change over time as business needs and external forces evolve.

DIMENSIONS OF DATA QUALITY

A *data quality dimension* is a measurable feature or characteristic of data. The term *dimension* is used to make the connection to dimensions in the measurement of physical objects (e.g., length, width, height). Data quality dimensions provide a vocabulary for defining data quality requirements. From there, they can be used to define results of initial data quality assessment as well as ongoing measurement. In order to measure the quality of data, an organization needs to establish characteristics that are not only important to business processes (worth measuring) but also measurable and actionable.

Dimensions provide a basis for measurable rules, which themselves should be directly connected to potential risks in critical processes. For example:

- **A risk**: If the data in the customer email address field is incomplete, then we will not be able to send product information to our customers via email, and we will lose potential sales.

- **A means of mitigating the risk**: We will measure the percentage of customers for whom we have usable email addresses, and we will improve our processes until we have a usable email address for at least 98% of our customers.

Many leading thinkers have written about data quality dimensions.[42] While there is not a single, agreed-to set of data quality dimensions, all sets contain common ideas. Dimensions include some characteristics that can be measured objectively (completeness, validity, format conformity) and others that depend on heavily context or on subjective interpretation (usability, reliability, reputation). Whatever names are used, dimensions focus on whether there is enough data (completeness), whether it is correct (accuracy, validity), how well it fits together (consistency, integrity, uniqueness), whether it is up-to-date (timeliness), accessible, usable, and secure.

In 2013, DAMA United Kingdom produced a white paper proposing six core dimensions of data quality. Their set included:

- **Completeness**: The proportion of data stored against the potential for 100%.

- **Uniqueness**: No entity instance (thing) will be recorded more than once based upon how that thing is identified.

- **Timeliness**: The degree to which data represent reality from the required point in time.

- **Validity**: Data is valid if it conforms to the syntax (format, type, range) of its definition.

- **Accuracy**: The degree to which data correctly describes the 'real world' object or event being described.

---

[42] See Strong and Wang (1996), Redman (1996, 2001), English (1999, 2008), Loshin (2001), Olson (2003), McGilvray (2008), and Sebastian-Coleman (2013) for detailed discussions on data quality dimensions. See Myers (2013) for a comparison of dimensions.

- **Consistency**: The absence of difference, when comparing two or more representations of a thing against a definition.

The DAMA UK white paper also describes other characteristics that have an impact on quality.

- **Usability**: Is the data understandable, relevant, accessible, maintainable and at the right level of precision?

- **Timing issues** (beyond timeliness itself): Is it stable yet responsive to legitimate change requests?

- **Flexibility**: Is the data comparable and compatible with other data? Does it have useful groupings and classifications? Can it be repurposed? Is it easy to manipulate?

- **Confidence**: Are data governance, data protection and data security in place? What is the reputation of the data, and is it verified or verifiable?

- **Value**: Is there a good cost / benefit case for the data? Is it being optimally used? Does it endanger people's safety or privacy or the legal responsibilities of the enterprise? Does it support or contradict the corporate image or the corporate message?

Any organization that wants to improve the quality of its data should adopt or develop a set of dimensions through which to measure quality. Coming to consensus about dimensions of quality can provide a starting point for a common vocabulary around quality.

DATA QUALITY MANAGEMENT

As noted above, sometimes the term *data quality* is used to refer to the processes used to measure or improve the quality of data.

These processes constitute *data quality management.* While all data management functions have the potential to impact the quality of data, the formal data quality management focuses on helping the organization:

- **Define high-quality data**, through DQ standards, rules, and requirements

- **Assess data** against those standards and communicate results to stakeholders

- **Monitor and report** on the quality of data in applications and data stores

- **Identify issues** and advocate for opportunities for improvement

Formal data quality management is similar to continuous quality management for other products. It includes managing data through its lifecycle by setting standards, building quality into the processes that create, transform, and store data, and measuring data against standards. Managing data to this level usually requires a data quality program team. The data quality program team is responsible for engaging both business and technical data management professionals and driving the work of applying quality management techniques to data to ensure that data is fit for consumption for a variety of purposes.

The team will likely be involved with a series of projects through which they can establish processes and best practices while addressing high priority data issues. Because managing the quality of data involves managing the data lifecycle, a data quality program will also have operational responsibilities related to data usage. For example, reporting on data quality levels, and engaging in the analysis, quantification, and prioritization of data issues.

The team is also responsible for working with those who need data to do their jobs to ensure the data meets their needs, and working with those who create, update, or delete data in the course of their jobs to ensure they are properly handling the data.

Data quality depends on all who interact with the data, not just data management professionals.

As is the case with data governance and with data management as a whole, data quality management is a program, not a project. It will include both project and maintenance work, along with a commitment to communications and training. Most importantly, the long-term success of data quality improvement program depends on getting an organization to change its culture and adopt a quality mindset. As stated in *The Leader's Data Manifesto*: fundamental, lasting change requires committed leadership and involvement from people at all levels in an organization. People who use data to do their jobs – which in most organizations is a very large percentage of employees – need to drive change. And one of the most critical changes to focus on is how their organizations manage and improve the quality of their data.[43]

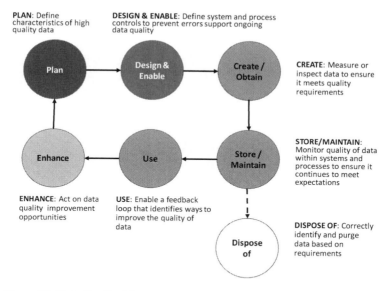

Figure 27: Data Quality Management and the Data Lifecycle (Adapted from DMBOK2, p. 29)

---

[43] For the full text of *The Leader's Data Manifesto*, see: https://bit.ly/2sQhcy7.

DAMA's data management principles assert that data management is management of the lifecycle of data and that managing data means managing the quality of data. Throughout the data lifecycle, data quality management activities help an organization define and measure expectations related to its data. These expectations may change over time as organizational uses of data evolve (see Figure 27).

DATA QUALITY AND OTHER DATA MANAGEMENT FUNCTIONS

As noted earlier, all areas of data management have the potential to affect the quality of data. Data governance and stewardship, data modeling, and Metadata management have direct effects on defining what high-quality data looks like. If these are not executed well, it is very difficult to have reliable data. The three are related in that they establish standards, definitions, and rules related to data. Data quality is about meeting expectations. Collectively, these describe a set of common expectations for quality.

The quality of data is based on how well it meets the requirements of data consumers. Having a robust process by which data is defined supports the ability of an organization to formalize and document the standards and requirements by which the quality of data can be measured.

Metadata defines what the data represents. Data Stewardship and the data modeling processes are sources of critical Metadata. Well-managed Metadata can also support the effort to improve the quality of data. A Metadata repository can house results of data quality measurements so that these are shared across the organization and the data quality team can work toward consensus about priorities and drivers for improvement.

A data quality program is more effective when part of a data governance program, not only because Data Stewardship is often aligned with data governance, but also because data quality issues are a primary reason for establishing enterprise-wide data governance. Incorporating data quality efforts into the overall governance effort enables the data quality program team to work with a range of stakeholders and enablers:

- Risk and security personnel who can help identify data-related organizational vulnerabilities

- Business process engineering and training staff who can help teams implement process improvements that increase efficiency and result in data more suitable for downstream uses

- Business and operational data stewards, and data owners who can identify critical data, define standards and quality expectations, and prioritize remediation of data issues

A Governance Organization can accelerate the work of a data quality program by:

- Setting priorities

- Developing and maintaining standards and policies for data quality

- Establishing communications and knowledge-sharing mechanisms

- Monitoring and reporting on performance and on data quality measurements

- Sharing data quality inspection results to build awareness and identify opportunities for improvement

Governance programs also often have responsibility for Master Data Management and Reference Data Management. It is worth noting that Master Data Management and Reference Data Management are both examples of processes focused on curating particular kinds of data for purposes of ensuring its quality.

Simply labeling a data set "Master Data" implies certain expectations about its content and reliability.

DATA QUALITY AND REGULATION

As noted in the chapter introduction, demonstrable data quality, like demonstrable data security, provides a competitive advantage. Customers and business partners alike expect and are beginning to demand complete and accurate data. Data quality is also a regulatory requirement in some cases. Data management practices can be audited. Regulations that are directly connected with data quality practices include examples noted previously:

- Sarbanes-Oxley (US) which focuses on the accuracy and validity of financial transactions

- Solvency II (EU) which focuses on data lineage and quality of data underpinning risk models

- General Data Protection Regulation (GDPR, EU) asserts that personal data must be accurate, and where necessary, kept up-to-date. Reasonable steps should be taken to erase or rectify inaccurate personal data.

- Personal Information Protection and Electronic Documents Act (PIPEDA, Canada) asserts that personal data must be as accurate, complete, and up-to-date for its purposes

It is worth noting that, even where data quality requirements are not specifically called out, the ability to protect personal data depends in part on that data being of high quality.

DATA QUALITY IMPROVEMENT CYCLE

Most approaches to improving data quality are based on the techniques of quality improvement in the manufacture of physical products.[44] In this paradigm, data is understood as the product of a set of processes. At its simplest, a process is defined as a series of steps that turns inputs into outputs. A process that creates data may consist of one step (data collection) or many steps: data collection, integration into a data warehouse, aggregation in a data mart, etc. At any step, data can be negatively affected. It can be collected incorrectly, dropped or duplicated between systems, aligned or aggregated incorrectly, etc.

Improving data quality requires the ability to assess the relationship between inputs and outputs to ensure inputs meet the requirements of the process and outputs conform to expectations. Since outputs from one process become inputs to other processes, requirements must be defined along the whole data chain.

A general approach to data quality improvement, shown in Figure 28, is a version of the Shewhart / Deming cycle[45]. Based on the scientific method, the Shewhart / Deming cycle is a problem-solving model known as 'plan-do-check-act'. Improvement comes through a defined set of steps. The condition of data must be measured against standards and, if it does not meet standards, root cause(s) of the discrepancy from standards must be identified and remediated. Root causes may be found in any of the steps of the process, technical or non-technical. Once remediated, data should be monitored to ensure that it continues to meet requirements.

---

44 See Wang (1998), English (1999), Redman (2001), Loshin (2001), and McGilvray (2008). See Pierce (2004) for an overview of literature related to the concept of data as a product.

45 See American Society for Quality: http://asq.org/learn-about-quality/project-planning-tools/overview/pdca-cycle.html Plan-Do-Check-Act was originated by Walter Shewhart and popularized by W. Edwards Deming. 6 Sigma's Measure, Analyze, Improve, Control (DMAIC) is a variation on this cycle.

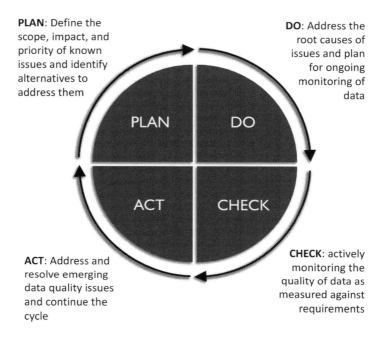

PLAN: Define the scope, impact, and priority of known issues and identify alternatives to address them

DO: Address the root causes of issues and plan for ongoing monitoring of data

ACT: Address and resolve emerging data quality issues and continue the cycle

CHECK: actively monitoring the quality of data as measured against requirements

Figure 28: A Data Quality Management Cycle based on the Shewhart Cycle (DMBOK2, p. 263)

For a given data set, a data quality improvement cycle begins by identifying the data that does not meet data consumers' requirements and data issues that are obstacles to the achievement of business objectives. Data needs to be assessed against key dimensions of quality and known business requirements. Root causes of issues will need to be identified so that stakeholders can understand the costs of remediation and the risks of not remediating the issues. This work is often done in conjunction with Data Stewards and other stakeholders.

In the *Plan* stage, the data quality team assesses the scope, impact, and priority of known issues, and evaluates alternatives to address them. This plan should be based on a solid foundation of analysis of the root causes of issues. From knowledge of the causes and the impact of the issues, cost / benefit can be understood, priority can be determined, and a basic plan can be formulated to address them.

In the *Do* stage, the DQ team leads efforts to address the root causes of issues and plan for ongoing monitoring of data. For root causes that are based on non-technical processes, the DQ team can work with process owners to implement changes. For root causes that require technical changes, the DQ team should work with technical teams and ensure that requirements are implemented correctly and that no unintended errors are introduced by technical changes.

The *Check* stage involves actively monitoring the quality of data as measured against requirements. As long as data meets defined thresholds for quality, additional actions are not required. The processes will be considered under control and meeting business requirements. However, if the data falls below acceptable quality thresholds, then additional action must be taken to bring it up to acceptable levels.

The *Act* stage is for activities to address and resolve emerging data quality issues. The cycle restarts, as the causes of issues are assessed and solutions proposed. Continuous improvement is achieved by starting a new cycle. New cycles begin as:

- Existing measurements fall below thresholds

- New data sets come under investigation

- New data quality requirements emerge for existing data sets

- Business rules, standards, or expectations change

Establishing criteria for data quality at the beginning of a process or system build is one sign of a mature data management organization. Doing so takes governance and discipline, as well as cross-functional collaboration.

Building quality into the data management processes from the beginning costs less than retrofitting it. Maintaining high-quality data throughout the data lifecycle is less risky than trying to improve quality in an existing process. It also creates a far lower impact on the organization.

It is best to do things right the first time, though few organizations have the luxury of doing so. Even if they do, managing quality is an ongoing process. Changing demands and organic growth over time can cause data quality issues that may be costly if unchecked, but can be nipped in the bud if an organization is attentive to the potential risks.

DATA QUALITY AND LEADERSHIP COMMITMENT

Data quality issues can emerge at any point in the data lifecycle, from creation to disposal. When investigating root causes, analysts should look for potential culprits, like problems with data entry, data processing, system design, and manual intervention in automated processes. Many issues will have multiple causes and contributing factors (especially if people have created ways to work around them). These causes of issues also imply that data quality issues can be prevented through:

- Improvement to interface design

- Testing of data quality rules as part of processing

- A focus on data quality within system design

- Strict controls on manual intervention in automated processes

Obviously, preventative tactics should be used. However, common sense says and research indicates that many data quality problems are caused by a lack of organizational commitment to high-quality data, which itself stems from a lack of leadership, in the form of both governance and management.

Every organization has information and data assets that are of value to its operations. Indeed, operations depend on the ability to share information. Despite this, few organizations manage these assets with rigor.

Many governance and information asset programs are driven solely by compliance, rather than by the potential value of data as an asset. A lack of recognition on the part of leadership means a lack of commitment within an organization to managing data as an asset, including managing its quality.[46] Barriers to the effective management of data quality (see Figure 29) include:[47]

- Lack of awareness on the part of leadership and staff

- Lack of business governance

- Lack of leadership and management

- Difficulty in justification of improvements

- Inappropriate or ineffective instruments to measure value

These barriers have negative effects on customer experience, productivity, morale, organizational effectiveness, revenue, and competitive advantage. They increase costs of running the organization and introduce risks as well.

As with understanding the root cause of any problem, recognition of these barriers – the root causes of poor quality data – gives an organization insight into how to improve its quality. If an organization realizes that it does not have strong business governance, ownership, and accountability, then it can address the problem by establishing business governance, ownership, and accountability. If leadership sees that the organization does not know how to put information to work, then leadership can put processes in place so that the organization can learn how to do so.

Recognition of a problem is the first step to solving it. Actually solving problems takes a lot of work. Most of the barriers to

---

[46] Evans & Price, 2012.

[47] Adapted from *The Leader's Data Manifesto*. https://dataleaders.org/.

managing information as an asset are cultural. Addressing them requires a formal process of organizational change management.

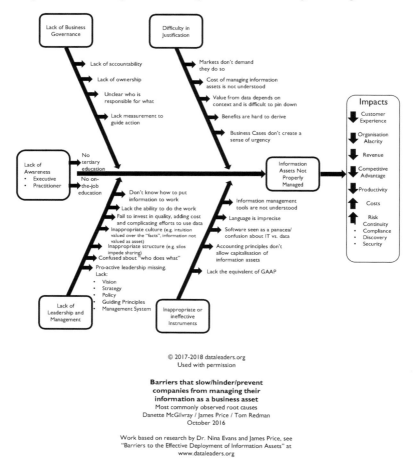

Figure 29: Barriers to Managing Information as a Business Asset (DMBOK2, p. 467) [48]

---

[48] Diagram developed by Danette McGilvray, James Price and Tom Redman. Used by permission. https://dataleaders.org/.

ORGANIZATION AND CULTURAL CHANGE

The quality of data will not be improved through a collection of tools and concepts, but through a mindset that helps employees and stakeholders to account for the quality of data needed to serve their organization and its customers. Getting an organization to be conscientious about data quality often requires significant cultural change. Such change requires vision and leadership.

The first step is promoting awareness about the role and importance of data to the organization and defining the characteristics of high-quality data. All employees must act responsibly and raise data quality issues, ask for good quality data as data consumers, and provide quality information to others. Every person who touches the data can impact the quality of that data. Data quality is not just the responsibility of a DQ team, a data governance team, or IT group.

Just as the employees need to understand the cost to acquire a new customer or retain an existing customer, they also need to know the organizational costs of poor quality data, as well as the conditions that cause data to be of poor quality. For example, if customer data is incomplete, a customer may receive the wrong product, creating direct and indirect costs to an organization. Not only will the customer return the product, but he or she may call and complain, using call center time, and creating the potential for reputational damage to the organization. If customer data is incomplete because the organization has not established clear requirements, then everyone who uses this data has a stake in clarifying requirements and following standards.

Ultimately, employees need to think and act differently if they are to produce better quality data and manage data in ways that ensures quality. This requires not only training but also reinforcement by committed leadership.

WHAT YOU NEED TO KNOW

- Poor quality data is costly. High-quality data has many benefits.

- The quality of data can be managed and improved, just as the quality of physical products can be managed and improved.

- The cost of getting data right the first time is lower than the cost of getting data wrong and fixing it.

- Data quality management requires a wide skill set and organizational commitment.

- Organizational commitment to quality requires committed leadership.

CHAPTER 12

What to do Now

Whether you have read the detail or skimmed the headings, at the point we hope you have a better understanding of the assertion in the Introduction that reliable data is not produced by accident. We have tried to show that well-managed data depends on planning, governance, and commitment to quality and security, as well as on disciplined execution of ongoing data management processes.

This chapter will discuss steps that are critical steps to initiate improvements to organizational maturity around data management. These include:

- Assessing current state

- Understanding options for improvement in order to develop a roadmap for data management

- Initiating an Organization Change Management program to support execution of the roadmap

ASSESS CURRENT STATE

The first step to solving a problem is understanding it. Before defining any new organization or attempting to improve an existing one, it is important to understand current state of component pieces, especially as these relate to culture, the existing operating model, and people. While the specifics of cultural change will differ from organization to organization, assessment of current state focused on improving data management will need to account for:

- **The role of data in the organization**: What key processes are data-driven? How are data requirements defined and understood? How well-recognized is the role that data plays in organizational strategy? In what ways is the organization aware of the costs of poor quality data?

- **Cultural norms about data**: Are there potential cultural obstacles to implementing or improving data management and governance structures? Are upstream business process owners aware of the downstream uses of their data?

- **Data management and data governance practices**: How and by whom is data-related work executed? How and by whom are decisions about data made?

- **How work is organized and executed**: What is the relation between project-focused and operational execution? What committee structures are in place that can support the data management effort? What is the operating model for IT/Business interactions? How are projects funded?

- **Reporting relationships**: Is the organization centralized or decentralized, hierarchical or flat? How collaborative are teams?

- **Skill levels**: What is the level of data knowledge and data management knowledge of Subject Matter Experts (SMEs) and other stakeholders, from line staff to executives?

Assessment of the current state should also include the level of satisfaction with the current state. This will provide insight into the organization's data management needs and priorities. For example:

- **Decision-making**: Does the organization have the information it needs to make sound, timely business decisions?

- **Reporting**: Does the organization have confidence in its revenue reports and other critical data?

- **Key Performance Indicators** (KPIs): How effectively does the organization track its KPIs?

- **Compliance**: Is the organization in compliance with all laws regarding management of data?

The most effective means to conduct such an assessment is by using a reliable data management maturity model that will provide insight into both how the organization compares with other organization and guidance on next steps.[49]

As described in Chapter 3, maturity models define five or six levels of maturity, each with its own characteristics, that span from non-existent or ad hoc to optimized or high performance.

---

[49] Adopting an appropriate maturity model is a key to success. See the DMBOK2 and: Alan McSweeney, *Review of Data Management Maturity Models*, SlideShare.net, published 2013-10-23. https://bit.ly/2spTCY9. Jeff Gorball, *Introduction to Data Management Maturity Models*, SlideShare.net, published 2016-08-01. McSweeney includes the DAMA-DMBOK as one of his maturity models, although the DMBOK is not structured as such.

The following generic summary of macro states of data management maturity illustrates the concept. A detailed assessment would include criteria for broad categories like people, processes and technology; and for sub-categories like strategy, policy, standards, role definition, technology / automation, etc. within each data management function or knowledge area.

- **Level 0: No Capability**: No organized data management practices or formal enterprise processes for managing data. Very few organizations exist at a Level 0. This level is acknowledged for purposes of definition.

- **Level 1 Initial / Ad Hoc**: General purpose data management using a limited tool set, with little or no governance. Data handling is highly reliant on a few experts. Roles and responsibilities are defined within silos. Each data owner receives, generates, and sends data autonomously. Controls, if they exist, are applied inconsistently. Solutions for managing data are limited. Data quality issues are pervasive and not addressed. Infrastructure supports are at the business unit level. Assessment criteria may include the presence of any process controls, such as logging of data quality issues.

- **Level 2 Repeatable**: Emergence of consistent tools and role definition to support process execution. In Level 2, the organization begins to use centralized tools and to provide more oversight for data management. Roles are defined and processes are not dependent solely on specific experts. There is organizational awareness of data quality issues and concepts. Concepts of Master and Reference Data Management begin to be recognized. Assessment criteria might include formal role definition in artifacts like job descriptions, the existence of process documentation, and the capacity to leverage tool sets.

- **Level 3 Defined**: Emerging data management capability. Level 3 sees the introduction and institutionalization of scalable data management processes and a view of data

management as an organizational enabler.
Characteristics include the replication of data across an
organization with some controls in place and a general
increase in overall data quality, along with coordinated
policy definition and management. More formal process
definition leads to a significant reduction in manual
intervention. This, along with a centralized design
process, means that process outcomes are more
predictable. Assessment criteria might include the
existence of data management policies, the use of
scalable processes, and the consistency of data models
and system controls.

- **Level 4 Managed**: Institutional knowledge gained from
  growth in Levels 1-3 enables the organization to predict
  results when approaching new projects and tasks and to
  begin to manage risks related to data. Data management
  includes performance metrics. Characteristics of Level 4
  include standardized tools for data management from
  desktop to infrastructure, coupled with a well-formed
  centralized planning and governance function.
  Expressions of this level are a measurable increase in
  data quality and organization-wide capabilities such as
  end-to-end data audits. Assessment criteria might
  include metrics related to project success, operational
  metrics for systems, and data quality metrics.

- **Level 5: Optimization**: When data management
  practices are optimized, they are highly predictable, due
  to process automation and technology change
  management. Organizations at this level of maturity
  focus on continuous improvement. At Level 5 tools
  enable a view of data across processes. The proliferation
  of data is controlled to prevent needless duplication.
  Well-understood metrics are used to manage and
  measure data quality and processes. Assessment criteria
  might include change management artifacts and metrics
  on process improvement.

Figure 30 illustrates one way of presenting a visual summary of findings from a DMMA. For each of the capabilities (Governance, Architecture, etc.) the outer ring of the display shows the level of capability the organization has determined it needs to compete successfully. The inner ring displays the level of capability as determined via the assessment. Areas where the distance between the two rings is largest represent the greatest risks to the organization. Such a report can help set priorities. It can also be used to measure progress over time.

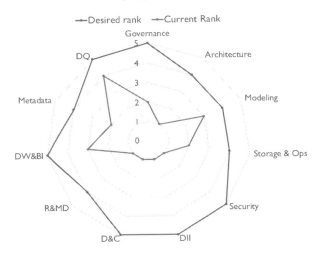

Figure 30: Example of a Data Management Maturity Assessment Visualization (DMBOK2, p. 537)

The primary goal of a current state assessment is to understand the organization's starting point in order to plan for improvement. An accurate evaluation is more important than a high score. A formal data management maturity evaluation places the organization on the maturity scale by clarifying specific strengths and weaknesses of critical data management activities. It helps the organization identify, prioritize, and implement improvement opportunities.

In meeting its primary goal, a DMMA can have a positive impact on culture. It helps:

- Educate stakeholders about data management concepts, principles, and practices
- Clarify stakeholder roles and responsibilities in relation to organizational data
- Highlight the need to manage data as a critical asset
- Broaden recognition of data management activities across the organization
- Contribute to improving the collaboration necessary for effective data governance

Based on assessment results, an organization can enhance its data management program so it supports the organization's operational and strategic direction. Typically, data management programs develop in organizational silos. They rarely begin with an enterprise view of the data. A DMMA can equip the organization to develop a cohesive vision that supports overall organizational strategy. A DMMA enables the organization to clarify priorities, crystalize objectives, and develop an integrated plan for improvement.

USE RESULTS TO PLAN FOR IMPROVEMENT

A current state assessment will help determine what is working well, what is not working well, and where an organization has gaps. Findings provide the basis for road-mapping program goals because they help determined where to start and how quickly to move forward. Goals should focus on:

- High-value improvement opportunities related to processes, methods, resources, and automation
- Capabilities that align with business strategy
- Governance processes for periodic evaluation of organizational progress based on characteristics in the model

The specifics of the action plans will depend on the results of the current state assessment, but an example will show how the process works.

Table 4 presents a very simplified model that accounts only for the adoption of a standard methodology and the degree of automation for the process.

Let's say an organization recognizes the need to improve the quality of its data. However, its current state assessment shows that it is at Level 1. It has not yet established repeatable practices around data quality measurement, but there are individuals who have tested the waters and figured some things out. Based on its overall strategy, it sets a goal to move from Level 1 to Level 3 within 18 months.

Achieving this goal requires an action plan that accounts for several streams of work:

- Researching approaches for measuring the quality of data and adopting an approach that aligns with the organization's pain points, measurement goals, and industry
- Training staff on the methodology
- Identifying and adopting tools to support execution of the methodology

In addition to executing plans to meet these goals, leaders should also account for future development (i.e., in moving to Level 3, the organization should also ready itself to move to Level 4).

This simple example shows the thought process around planning for improvement of one component of data management. As noted in Chapter 3, Data Management Maturity Assessments can have different focus areas. If your organization comprehensively evaluates its data management practices, then the output will identify many opportunities for improvement. These will need to be prioritized to support business strategy.

Fortunately, a data management maturity model will include built-in guidance, by describing what progress looks like within and across data management functional areas. The stage-based path to improvement can be tailored to an organization's needs and priorities.

Maturity Level	DQ Measurement Characteristics	Degree of Automation
Level 5 Optimized: Process improvement goals are quantified	DQ reports are widely shared among management stakeholders. Results from data quality measurement are used to identify opportunities for system and business process improvements and the impact of these improvements is reported on.	Reporting, including alerts, is fully automated
Level 4 Managed: Processes are quantified and controlled	System and business process owners are required to measure the quality of their data and report on results so that data consumers have consistent knowledge of the quality of data.	The process for measurement is fully automated.
Level 3 Defined: Standards are set and used	Standards are defined for data quality measurement and are being applied across teams.	A standard approach to automation has been adopted.
Level 2 Repeatable: Minimum process discipline is in place	People have learned approaches to measuring the quality of data and they are developing consistent approaches to doing so.	Processes are still largely manual, but some teams have tested automation.
Level 1 Initial or Ad Hoc: Success depends on the competence of individuals	Individuals are trying to measure the quality of data, but doing so is not directly part of their jobs and they do not have a defined methodology.	None. Measurements are taken manually
Level 0 Absence of capability	Data quality measurement does not exist.	Not applicable

Table 4: Maturity Levels for Data Quality Measurement

INITIATE ORGANIZATIONAL CHANGE MANAGEMENT TO SUPPORT THE ROADMAP

Most organizations that seek to improve their data management or governance practices are in the middle of the capability maturity scale (i.e., they are neither 0's nor 5's on the maturity scale). Which means almost all of them need to improve their practices.

For most organizations, improving data management practices requires changing how people work together and how they understand the role of data in their organizations, as well as the way they use data and deploy technology to support organizational processes. Successful data management practices require, among other factors:

- Learning to manage on the horizontal by aligning accountabilities along the information value chain

- Changing focus from vertical (silo) accountability to shared stewardship of information

- Evolving information quality from a niche business concern or the job of the IT department into a core value of the organization

- Shifting thinking about information quality from 'data cleansing and scorecards' to a more fundamental organizational capability of building quality into processes

- Implementing processes to measure the cost of poor data management and the value of disciplined data management

This level of change is not achieved through technology (even though appropriate use of software tools can support delivery). It is instead realized through a careful and structured approach to the management of change in the organization. Change will be required at all levels. It is critical that it is managed and coordinated so as to avoid dead-end initiatives, loss of trust, and damage to the credibility of the information management function and its leadership.

Cultural change requires planning, training, and reinforcement. Awareness, ownership, and accountability are key to activating and engaging people in data management initiatives, policies, and processes.

Critical success factors for organizational change management are well-known. Ten factors have been consistently shown to play a key role in the success of effective data management organizations, regardless of their structure:

1. **Executive sponsorship**: The executive sponsor should understand and believe in the initiative. He or she must be able to effectively engage other leaders in support of the changes.

2. **Clear vision**: Organizational leaders must ensure that all stakeholders who are affected by data management – both internal and external – understand and internalize what data management is, why it is important, and how their work will affect and be affected by it.

3. **Proactive change management**: Applying organizational change management to the establishment of a data management practice addresses the people challenges and increases the likelihood that desired practices and organizational structures are sustainable over time.

4. **Leadership alignment**: Leadership alignment ensures that there is agreement on – and unified support for – the need for a data management program and that there is agreement on how success will be defined. Leadership alignment includes both the alignment between the leaders' goals and the data management outcomes and value *and* alignment in purpose amongst the leaders.

5. **Communication**: The organization must ensure that stakeholders have a clear understanding of what data management is and why it is important to the company, what is changing, and what changes in behavior are required.

6. **Stakeholder engagement**: Individuals, as well as groups, affected by a data management initiative will react differently to the new program and their role within it. How the organization engages these stakeholders – how they communicate with, respond to, and involve them – will have a significant impact on the success of the initiative.

7. **Orientation and training**: Education is essential to making data management happen. Different groups of people (leaders, data stewards, data owners, technical teams) will require different types and levels of education so they can perform their roles effectively. Many people will require training on new policies, processes, techniques, procedures, and even tools.

8. **Adoption measurement**: Build metrics around the progress and adoption of the data management guidelines and plan to know that the data management roadmap is working and that it will continue working. The enabling aspect of data management could focus on the improvement of data-centric processes, such as month-end closing, identification of risk, and efficiency of project execution. The innovation aspect of data management could focus on improvement in decision-making and analytics through improved and trusted data.

9. **Adherence to guiding principles**: Guiding principles, such as DAMA's principles of data management, serve as the reference points from which all decisions will be made. Establishing them is an important first step in creating a data management program that effectively drives changes in behavior.

10. **Evolution not revolution**: In all aspects of data management, the philosophy of 'evolution not revolution' helps to minimize big changes or large scale high risk projects. Establishing an organization that evolves and matures over time, incrementally improving the way that data is managed and prioritized by business objectives, will ensure that new policies and processes are adopted and behavioral change is sustained.

WHAT YOU NEED TO KNOW

- Even though data management is complex, it can be executed effectively and efficiently.

- In your leadership role, you can make a significant contribution to your organization's ability to get value from its data, if you show and share commitment to the process.

- Moving forward starts by being smart about current state: Do an assessment that allows you to understand where you are and plan from there.

- Recognize that changes in how you manage data will change how people work together. Do formal change management to achieve the cultural changes that will bring about success.

- Follow principles and best practices as you clear the way for your organization to get more value from its data.

Acknowledgements

This book is based on the second edition of DAMA's Data Management Body of Knowledge (DMBOK2). It could not have been written without the primary contributors to the DMBOK2 and the initial editorial board who compiled the DMBOK2 manuscript and integrated feedback from hundreds of DAMA members.

Contributors and editors include: Robert Abate, Gene Boomer, Chris Bradley, Micheline Casey, Mark Cowan, Pat Cupoli, Susan Earley, Håkan Edvinsson, Deborah Henderson, Steve Hoberman, Ken Kring, Krish Krishnan, John Ladley, Lisa Nelson, Daragh O Brien, Kelle O'Neal, Katherine O'Keefe, Mehmet Orun, April Reeve, David Schlesinger (CISSP), Sanjay Shirude, Eva Smith, Martin Sykora, Elena Sykora, Rossano Tavares, Andrea Thomsen, and Saad Yacu.

The idea for an executive guide to data management was the brainchild of DAMA International President Sue Geuens. It would not have come into being without her initiative and encouragement. Steve Hoberman, DMBOK publisher and data modeling rock star, has, once again, provided invaluable advice and guidance during the process of working on this book.

Special thanks to my husband, George Sebastian-Coleman for his support, encouragement, and … patience.

Laura Sebastian-Coleman, Ph.D., CDM, IQCP
VP Publications and Editorial Services
DAMA International

References

Abernethy, Kenneth and J. Thomas Allen. *Exploring the Digital Domain: An Introduction to Computers and Information Fluency.* 2nd ed., 2004. Print.

Ackerman Anderson, Linda and Dean Anderson. *The Change Leader's Roadmap and Beyond Change Management.* 2nd ed. Pfeiffer, 2010. Print.

Adelman, Sid, Larissa Moss, and Majid Abai. *Data Strategy.* Addison-Wesley Professional, 2005. Print.

Afflerbach, Peter. *Essential Readings on Assessment.* International Reading Association, 2010. Print.

Ahlemann, Frederik, Eric Stettiner, Marcus Messerschmidt, and Christine Legner, editors. *Strategic Enterprise Architecture Management: Challenges, Best Practices, and Future Developments.* Springer, 2012. Print.

Aiken, Peter and Juanita Billings. *Monetizing Data Management: Finding the Value in your Organization's Most Important Asset.* Technics Publications, LLC, 2014. Print.

Aiken, Peter and Michael M. Gorman. *The Case for the Chief Data Officer: Recasting the C-Suite to Leverage Your Most Valuable Asset.* Morgan Kaufmann, 2013. Print.

Aiken, Peter and Todd Harbour. *Data Strategy and the Enterprise Executive.* Technics Publishing, LLC, 2017. Print.

Allen, Mark and Dalton Cervo. *Multi-Domain Master Data Management: Advanced MDM and Data Governance in Practice.* Morgan Kaufmann, 2015. Print.

Anderson, Carl. *Creating a Data-Driven Organization.* O'Reilly Media, 2015. Print.

Andress, Jason. *The Basics of Information Security: Understanding the Fundamentals of InfoSec in Theory and Practice.* Syngress, 2011. Print.

Armistead, Leigh. *Information Operations Matters: Best Practices.* Potomac Books Inc., 2010. Print.

Arthur, Lisa. *Big Data Marketing: Engage Your Customers More Effectively and Drive Value.* Wiley, 2013.

Barksdale, Susan and Teri Lund. *10 Steps to Successful Strategic Planning.* ASTD, 2006. Print.

Barlow, Mike. *Real-Time Big Data Analytics: Emerging Architecture.* O'Reilly Media, 2013.

Baskarada, Sasa. *IQM-CMM: Information Quality Management Capability Maturity Model.* Vieweg+Teubner Verlag, 2009. Print.

Batini, Carlo, and Monica Scannapieco. *Data Quality: Concepts, Methodologies and Techniques.* Springer, 2006. Print.

Bean, Randy. "The Chief Data Officer Dilemma". Forbes, 29 January 2018. Retrieved from https://bit.ly/2J8ahVZ.

Becker, Ethan F. and Jon Wortmann. *Mastering Communication at Work: How to Lead, Manage, and Influence.* McGraw-Hill, 2009. Print.

Bernard, Scott A. *An Introduction to Enterprise Architecture.* 2nd ed., Authorhouse, 2005. Print.

Berson, Alex and Larry Dubov. *Master Data Management and Customer Data Integration for a Global Enterprise.* McGraw-Hill, 2007. Print.

Bevan, Richard. *Changemaking: Tactics and resources for managing organizational change.* CreateSpace Independent Publishing Platform, 2011. Print.

Biere, Mike. *The New Era of Enterprise Business Intelligence: Using Analytics to Achieve a Global Competitive Advantage.* IBM Press, 2010. Print.

Blann, Andrew. *Data Handling and Analysis*. Oxford University Press, 2015. Print.

Blokdijk, Gerard. *Stakeholder Analysis - Simple Steps to Win, Insights and Opportunities for Maxing Out Success*. Complete Publishing, 2015. Print.

Boiko, Bob. *Content Management Bible*. 2nd ed., Wiley, 2004. Print.

Borek, Alexander et al. *Total Information Risk Management: Maximizing the Value of Data and Information Assets*. Morgan Kaufmann, 2013. Print.

Boutros, Tristan and Tim Purdie. *The Process Improvement Handbook: A Blueprint for Managing Change and Increasing Organizational Performance*. McGraw-Hill Education, 2013. Print.

Brackett, Michael H. *Data Resource Design: Reality Beyond Illusion*. Technics Publications, LLC, 2012.

Brennan, Michael. "Can computers be racist? Big data, inequality, and discrimination." Ford Foundation Equals Change, 18 November 2015. Retrieved from https://bit.ly/1Om41ap.

Brestoff, Nelson E. and William H. Inmon. *Preventing Litigation: An Early Warning System to Get Big Value Out of Big Data*. Business Expert Press, 2015. Print.

Bridges, William. *Managing Transitions: Making the Most of Change*. Da Capo Lifelong Books, 2009.

Bryce, Tim. "Benefits of a Data Taxonomy." Toolbox Tech, 11 July 2005. Retrieved from http://it.toolbox.com/blogs/irm-blog/the-benefits-of-a-data-taxonomy-4916.

Brzezinski, Robert. *HIPAA Privacy and Security Compliance - Simplified: Practical Guide for Healthcare Providers and Practice Managers*. CreateSpace Independent Publishing Platform, 2014. Print.

Carstensen, Jared, Bernard Golden, and JP Morgenthal. *Cloud Computing - Assessing the Risks*. IT Governance Publishing, 2012. Print.

Cassell, Kay Ann and Uma Hiremath. *Reference and Information Services: An Introduction*. 3d ed., ALA Neal-Schuman, 2012. Print.

Center for Creative Leadership (CCL), Talula Cartwright, and David Baldwin. *Communicating Your Vision.* Pfeiffer, 2007. Print.

Chisholm, Malcolm and Roblyn-Lee, Diane. *Definitions in Data Management: A Guide to Fundamental Semantic Metadata.* Design Media, 2008. Print.

Chisholm, Malcolm. *Managing Reference Data in Enterprise Databases: Binding Corporate Data to the Wider World.* Morgan Kaufmann, 2000. Print.

CMMI Institute. http://cmmiinstitute.com/data-management-maturity.

Cokins, Gary et al. *CIO Best Practices: Enabling Strategic Value with Information Technology.* 2nd ed., Wiley, 2010. Print.

Collier, Ken W. *Agile Analytics: A Value-Driven Approach to Business Intelligence and Data Warehousing.* Addison-Wesley Professional, 2011. Print.

Confessore, Nicholas and Danny Hakim. "Data Firm says 'Secret Sauce' Aided Trump; Many Scoff." New York Times, 6 March 2017. Retrieved from https://nyti.ms/2J2aDx2.

Contreras, Melissa. *People Skills for Business: Winning Social Skills That Put You Ahead of the Competition.* CreateSpace Independent Publishing Platform, 2013. Print.

Council for Big Data, Ethics, and Society. http://bdes.datasociety.net/

Curley, Martin, Jim Kenneally, and Marian Carcary (editors). *IT Capability Maturity Framework IT-CMF.* Van Haren Publishing, 2015. Print.

DAMA International. *The DAMA Data Management Body of Knowledge (DMBOK2).* 2nd ed., Technics Publications, LLC, 2017. Print.

DAMA International. *The DAMA Dictionary of Data Management.* 2nd ed., Technics Publications, LLC, 2011. Print.

Darrow, Barb. "Is Big Data Killing Democracy?" Fortune Magazine, 15 September 2017. Retrieved from http://fortune.com/2017/09/15/election-data-democracy/.

Data Leader. https://dataleaders.org.

Davenport, Thomas H. *Big Data at Work: Dispelling the Myths, Uncovering the Opportunities.* Harvard Business Review Press, 2014. Print.

Davis, Kord. *Ethics of Big Data: Balancing Risk and Innovation.* O'Reilly Media, 2012. Print.

Dean, Jared. *Big Data, Data Mining, and Machine Learning: Value Creation for Business Leaders and Practitioners.* Wiley, 2014. Print.

Doan, AnHai, Alon Halevy, and Zachary Ives. *Principles of Data Integration.* Morgan Kaufmann, 2012.

Dwivedi, Himanshu. *Securing Storage: A Practical Guide to SAN and NAS Security.* Addison-Wesley Professional, 2005. Print.

Dyche, Jill and Evan Levy. *Customer Data Integration: Reaching a Single Version of the Truth.* John Wiley & Sons, 2006. Print.

Eckerson, Wayne W. *Performance Dashboards: Measuring, Monitoring, and Managing Your Business.* Wiley, 2005. Print.

Edvinsson, Håkan and Lottie Aderinne. *Enterprise Architecture Made Simple: Using the Ready, Set, Go Approach to Achieving Information Centricity.* Technics Publications, LLC, 2013. Print.

EMC Education Services, ed. *Data Science and Big Data Analytics: Discovering, Analyzing, Visualizing and Presenting Data.* Wiley, 2015. Print.

English, Larry. *Improving Data Warehouse and Business Information Quality: Methods For Reducing Costs And Increasing Profits.* John Wiley & Sons, 1999. Print.

English, Larry. *Information Quality Applied: Best Practices for Improving Business Information, Processes, and Systems.* Wiley Publishing, 2009. Print.

Evans, Nina and Price, James. "Barriers to the Effective Deployment of Information Assets: An Executive Management Perspective." Interdisciplinary Journal of Information, Knowledge, and Management, Volume 7, 2012. Retrieved from https://dataleaders.org/.

Executive Office of the President, National Science and Technology Council Committee on Technology. "Preparing for the Future of Artificial Intelligence." National Archives, October 2016. Retrieved from https://bit.ly/2j3XA4k.

Federal Trade Commission, US (FTC). "Federal Trade Commission Report Protecting Consumer Privacy in an Era of Rapid Change." March 2012. Retrieved from https://bit.ly/2rVgTxQ.

Fisher, Craig, Eitel Lauría, Shobha Chengalur-Smith, and Richard Wang. *Introduction to Information Quality*. M.I.T. Information Quality Program Publications, 2006. Print.

Fisher, Tony. *The Data Asset: How Smart Companies Govern Their Data for Business Success*. Wiley, 2009. Print.

Foreman, John W. *Data Smart: Using Data Science to Transform Information into Insight*. Wiley, 2013.

Freund, Jack and Jack Jones. *Measuring and Managing Information Risk: A FAIR Approach*. Butterworth-Heinemann, 2014. Print.

Fuster, Gloria González. "The Emergence of Personal Data Protection as a Fundamental Right of the EU." Springer, 2014. Print.

Gartner, Tom McCall, contributor. "Understanding the Chief Data Officer Role." 18 February 2015. Retrieved from https://gtnr.it/1RIDKa6.

Regulation (EU) 2016/679 of the European Parliament and of the Council of 27 April 2016 on the protection of natural persons with regard to the processing of personal data and on the free movement of such data, and repealing Directive 95/46/EC (General Data Protection Regulation). Retrieved from http://data.europa.eu/eli/reg/2016/679/oj.

Gemignani, Zach, et al. *Data Fluency: Empowering Your Organization with Effective Data Communication*. Wiley, 2014. Print.

Ghavami, Peter PhD. *Big Data Governance: Modern Data Management Principles for Hadoop, NoSQL & Big Data Analytics*. CreateSpace Independent Publishing Platform, 2015. Print.

Gibbons, Paul. *The Science of Successful Organizational Change: How Leaders Set Strategy, Change Behavior, and Create an Agile Culture*. Pearson FT Press, 2015. Print.

Giordano, Anthony David. *Performing Information Governance: A Step-by-step Guide to Making Information Governance Work.* IBM Press, 2014. Print.

Hagan, Paula J., ed. *EABOK: Guide to the (Evolving) Enterprise Architecture Body of Knowledge.* MITRE Corporation, 2004. Retrieved from https://bit.ly/2HisN1m.

Halpin, Terry. *Information Modeling and Relational Databases: From Conceptual Analysis to Logical Design.* Morgan Kaufmann, 2001. Print.

Harkins, Malcolm. *Managing Risk and Information Security: Protect to Enable (Expert's Voice in Information Technology).* Apress, 2012.

Harrison, Michael I. *Diagnosing Organizations: Methods, Models, and Processes.* 3rd ed., SAGE Publications, Inc., 2004. Print.

Hasselbalch, Gry and Pernille Tranberg. *Data Ethics: The New Competitive Advantage.* Publishare, 2016.

Hay, David C. *Data Model Patterns: A Metadata Map.* Morgan Kaufmann, 2006. Print.

Hayden, Lance. *IT Security Metrics: A Practical Framework for Measuring Security & Protecting Data.* McGraw-Hill Osborne Media, 2010. Print.

Hiatt, Jeffrey and Timothy Creasey. *Change Management: The People Side of Change.* Prosci Learning Center Publications, 2012. Print.

Hillard, Robert. *Information-Driven Business: How to Manage Data and Information for Maximum Advantage.* Wiley, 2010. Print.

Hoberman, Steve, Donna Burbank, and Chris Bradley. *Data Modeling for the Business: A Handbook for Aligning the Business with IT using High-Level Data Models.* Technics Publications, LLC, 2009. Print.

Holman, Peggy, Tom Devane, Steven Cady. *The Change Handbook: The Definitive Resource on Today's Best Methods for Engaging Whole Systems.* 2nd ed. Berrett-Koehler Publishers, 2007. Print.

Hoogervorst, Jan A. P. *Enterprise Governance and Enterprise Engineering.* Springer, 2009. Print.

Howson, Cindi. *Successful Business Intelligence: Unlock the Value of BI & Big Data*. 2nd ed., Mcgraw-Hill Osborne Media, 2013. Print.

Inmon (Website) https://bit.ly/1FtgeIL.

Inmon, W. *Building the Data Warehouse*. 4th ed., Wiley, 2005. Print.

Inmon, W. H., Claudia Imhoff, and Ryan Sousa. *The Corporate Information Factory*. 2nd ed., John Wiley & Sons, 2000. Print.

Inmon, W.H., and Dan Linstedt. *Data Architecture: A Primer for the Data Scientist: Big Data, Data Warehouse and Data Vault*. 1st ed., Morgan Kaufmann, 2014.

Jensen, David. "Data Snooping, Dredging and Fishing: The Dark Side of Data Mining A SIGKDD99 Panel Report." ACM SIGKDD, Vol. 1, Issue 2. January 2000. Retrieved from http://ftp.bstu.by/ai/Data-mining/Stock-market/expl99.pdf.

Johnson, Deborah G. *Computer Ethics*. 4th ed., Pearson, 2009. Print.

Jugulum, Rajesh. *Competing with High Quality Data*. Wiley, 2014. Print.

Kark, Khalid. "Building a Business Case for Information Security". Computer World, 10 August 2009. Retrieved from https://bit.ly/2qFyjk2.

Kaunert, C. and S. Leonard, eds. *European Security, Terrorism and Intelligence: Tackling New Security Challenges in Europe*. Palgrave Macmillan, 2013. Print.

Kennedy, Gwen, and Leighton Peter Prabhu. *Data Privacy: A Practical Guide*. Interstice Consulting LLP, 2014.

Kent, William. *Data and Reality: A Timeless Perspective on Perceiving and Managing Information in Our Imprecise World*. 3d ed., Technics Publications, LLC, 2012. Print.

Kimball, Ralph, and Margy Ross. *The Data Warehouse Toolkit: The Definitive Guide to Dimensional Modeling*. 3d ed., Wiley, 2013. Print.

Kitchin, Rob. *The Data Revolution: Big Data, Open Data, Data Infrastructures and Their Consequences*. SAGE Publications Ltd., 2014. Print.

Kotter, John P. *Leading Change*. Harvard Business Review Press, 2012. Print.

Kring, Kenneth L. *Business Strategy Mapping - The Power of Knowing How it All Fits Together*. Langdon Street Press, 2009. Print.

Krishnan, Krish. *Data Warehousing in the Age of Big Data*. Morgan Kaufmann, 2013. Print.

Ladley, John. *Data Governance: How to Design, Deploy and Sustain an Effective Data Governance Program*. Morgan Kaufmann, 2012. Print.

Ladley, John. *Making Enterprise Information Management (EIM) Work for Business: A Guide to Understanding Information as an Asset*. Morgan Kaufmann, 2010. Print.

Lake, Peter and Robert Drake. *Information Systems Management in the Big Data Era*. Springer, 2015.

Lambe, Patrick. *Organising Knowledge: Taxonomies, Knowledge and Organisational Effectiveness*. Chandos Publishing, 2007. Print.

Laney, Doug. "3D Data Management: Controlling Data Volume, Velocity, and Variety." The Meta Group, 6 February 2001. Retrieved from https://gtnr.it/1bKflKH.

Laney, Douglas, *Infonomics: How to Monetize, Manage, and Measure Information as an Asset for Competitive Advantage*. Gartner, 2018.

Lankhorst, Marc. *Enterprise Architecture at Work: Modeling, Communication and Analysis*. Springer, 2005. Print.

Lee, Yang W., Leo L. Pipino, James D. Funk, and Richard Y. Wang. *Journey to Data Quality*. The MIT Press, 2006. Print.

Lipschultz, Jeremy Harris. *Social Media Communication: Concepts, Practices, Data, Law and Ethics*. Routledge, 2014. Print.

Loh, Steve. *Data-ism: The Revolution Transforming Decision Making, Consumer Behavior, and Almost Everything Else*. HarperBusiness, 2015. Print.

Loshin, David. *Enterprise Knowledge Management: The Data Quality Approach*. Morgan Kaufmann, 2001. Print.

Loshin, David. *Master Data Management*. Morgan Kaufmann, 2009. Print.

Loukides, Mike. *What Is Data Science?* O'Reilly Media, 2012.

Luecke, Richard. *Managing Change and Transition*. Harvard Business Review Press, 2003. Print.

Martin, James and Joe Leben. *Strategic Information Planning Methodologies*. 2nd ed., Prentice Hall, 1989. Print.

Marz, Nathan and James Warren. *Big Data: Principles and best practices of scalable realtime data systems*. Manning Publications, 2015. Print.

Maydanchik, Arkady. *Data Quality Assessment*. Technics Publications, LLC, 2007. Print.

Mayfield, M.I. *On Handling the Data*. CreateSpace Independent Publishing Platform, 2015. Print.

McCandless, David. *Information is Beautiful*. Collins, 2012.

McGilvray, Danette. *Executing Data Quality Projects: Ten Steps to Quality Data and Trusted Information*. Morgan Kaufmann, 2008. Print.

McKnight, William. *Information Management: Strategies for Gaining a Competitive Advantage with Data*. Morgan Kaufmann, 2013. Print.

McSweeney, Alan. *Review of Data Management Maturity Models*. SlideShare, 23 October 2013. Retrieved from https://bit.ly/2spTCY9.

Moody, Daniel and Walsh, Peter. "Measuring The Value of Information: An Asset Valuation Approach." European Conference on Information Systems (ECIS), 1999. Retrieved from https://bit.ly/29JucLO.

Myers, Dan. "The Value of Using the Dimensions of Data Quality." Information Management, August 2013. Retrieved from https://bit.ly/2tsMYiA.

National Institute for Standards and Technology (US Department of Commerce). "Cybersecurity Framework." Retrieved from https://bit.ly/1eQYolG.

Nichols, Kevin. *Enterprise Content Strategy: A Project Guide*. XML Press, 2015. Print.

O'Keefe, Katherine and Daragh O Brien. *Ethical Data and Information Management*. Kogan Page, 2018.

Olson, Jack E. *Data Quality: The Accuracy Dimension*. Morgan Kaufmann, 2003. Print.

Park, Jung-ran, editor. *Metadata Best Practices and Guidelines: Current Implementation and Future Trends*. Routledge, 2014. Print.

Plotkin, David. *Data Stewardship: An Actionable Guide to Effective Data Management and Data Governance*. Morgan Kaufmann, 2013. Print.

Pomerantz, Jeffrey. *Metadata*. The MIT Press, 2015. Print.

PROSCI. "ADKAR: Why it Works." Retrieved from https://bit.ly/2tt1bf9.

Provost, Foster and Tom Fawcett. *Data Science for Business: What you need to know about data mining and data-analytic thinking*. O'Reilly Media, 2013. Print.

Quinn, Michael J. *Ethics for the Information Age*. 6th ed., Pearson, 2014. Print.

Redman, Thomas. "Bad Data Costs U.S. $3 Trillion per Year." Harvard Business Review, 22 September 2016.

Redman, Thomas. *Data Driven: Profiting from Your Most Important Business Asset*. Harvard Business Review Press, 2008. Print.

Redman, Thomas. *Data Quality: The Field Guide*. Digital Press, 2001. Print.

Redman, Thomas. *Getting in Front on Data*. Technics Publishing, LLC, 2017.

Reeve, April. *Managing Data in Motion: Data Integration Best Practice Techniques and Technologies*. Morgan Kaufmann, 2013. Print.

Reeves, Laura L. *A Manager's Guide to Data Warehousing*. Wiley, 2009. Print.

Reid, Roger, Gareth Fraser-King, and W. David Schwaderer. *Data Lifecycles: Managing Data for Strategic Advantage*. Wiley, 2007. Print.

Reinke, Guido. *The Regulatory Compliance Matrix: Regulation of Financial Services, Information and Communication Technology, and Generally Related Matters*. GOLD RUSH Publishing, 2015. Print.

Rhoton, John. *Cloud Computing Explained: Implementation Handbook for Enterprises*. Recursive Press, 2009. Print.

Russell, Matthew A. *Mining the Social Web: Data Mining Facebook, Twitter, LinkedIn, Google+, GitHub, and More*. 2nd ed., O'Reilly Media, 2013. Print.

Salminen, Joni and Valtteri Kaartemo, eds. *Big Data: Definitions, Business Logics, and Best Practices to Apply in Your Business*. Amazon Digital Services, Inc., 2014.

Schmarzo, Bill. *Big Data MBA: Driving Business Strategies with Data Science*. Wiley, 2015. Print.

Sebastian-Coleman, Laura. *Measuring Data Quality for Ongoing Improvement: A Data Quality Assessment Framework*. Morgan Kaufmann, 2013. Print.

Seiner, Robert S. *Non-Invasive Data Governance*. Technics Publishing, LLC, 2014. Print.

Sherman, Rick. *Business Intelligence Guidebook: From Data Integration to Analytics*. Morgan Kaufmann, 2014. Print.

Simon, Alan. *Modern Enterprise Business Intelligence and Data Management: A Roadmap for IT Directors, Managers, and Architects*. Morgan Kaufmann, 2014. Print.

Simsion, Graeme. *Data Modeling: Theory and Practice*. Technics Publications, LLC, 2007. Print.

Singer, P.W. and Allan Friedman. *Cybersecurity and Cyberwar: What Everyone Needs to Know®*. Oxford University Press, 2014. Print.

Smallwood, Robert F. *Information Governance: Concepts, Strategies, and Best Practices.* Wiley, 2014. Print.

Soares, Sunil. *Selling Information Governance to the Business: Best Practices by Industry and Job Function.* MC Press, 2011. Print.

Soares, Sunil. *The Chief Data Officer Handbook for Data Governance.* MC Press, 2015. Print.

Spewak, Steven and Steven C. Hill. *Enterprise Architecture Planning: Developing a Blueprint for Data, Applications, and Technology.* 2nd ed., Wiley-QED , 1993. Print.

Surdak, Christopher. *Data Crush: How the Information Tidal Wave is Driving New Business Opportunities.* AMACOM , 2014. Print.

Talburt, John and Yinle Zhou. *Entity Information Management Lifecycle for Big Data.* Morgan Kauffman, 2015. Print.

Talburt, John. *Entity Resolution and Information Quality.* Morgan Kaufmann, 2011. Print.

Tarantino, Anthony. *The Governance, Risk, and Compliance Handbook: Technology, Finance, Environmental, and International Guidance and Best Practices.* Wiley, 2008. Print.

The Data Governance Institute (Web site). https://bit.ly/1ef0tnb.

Thomas, Liisa M. *Thomas On Data Breach: A Practical Guide to Handling Data Breach Notifications Worldwide.* LegalWorks, 2015. Print.

Tufte, Edward R. *The Visual Display of Quantitative Information.* 2nd ed., Graphics Press, 2001. Print.

US Department of Commerce. *Guidelines on Security and Privacy in Public Cloud Computing.* CreateSpace Independent Publishing Platform, 2014. Print.

US Department of Defense. *Information Operations: Doctrine, Tactics, Techniques, and Procedures.* 2011.

US Department of Health and Human Services. "The Belmont Report." 1979. Retrieved from https://bit.ly/2tNjb3u.

US Department of Homeland Security. "Applying Principles to Information and Communication Technology Research: A Companion to the Department of Homeland Security Menlo Report". 3 January 2012. Retrieved from https://bit.ly/2rV2mSR.

van der Lans, Rick. *Data Virtualization for Business Intelligence Systems: Revolutionizing Data Integration for Data Warehouses.* Morgan Kaufmann, 2012. Print.

van Rijmenam, Mark. *Think Bigger: Developing a Successful Big Data Strategy for Your Business.* AMACOM, 2014. Print.

Verhoef, Peter C., Edwin Kooge, and Natasha Walk. *Creating Value with Big Data Analytics: Making Smarter Marketing Decisions.* Routledge, 2016. Print.

Vitt, Elizabeth, Michael Luckevich, and Stacia Misner. *Business Intelligence.* Microsoft Press, 2008. Print.

Waclawski, Janine. *Organization Development: A Data-Driven Approach to Organizational Change.* Pfeiffer, 2001. Print.

Warden, Pete. *Big Data Glossary.* O'Reilly Media, 2011. Print.

Williams, Branden R. and Anton Chuvakin Ph.D. *PCI Compliance: Understand and Implement Effective PCI Data Security Standard Compliance.* 4th ed., Syngress, 2014. Print.

Zeng, Marcia Lei and Jian Qin. *Metadata.* 2nd ed., ALA Neal-Schuman, 2015. Print.

Index

Made in the USA
Columbia, SC
25 May 2022